MW00775129

PRAISE FOR *DISRUPTABLE*

"Allan is a lifelong entrepreneur and radical thinker who is no stranger to disruptive ideas. The concepts in *Disruptable* force the reader to break out of traditional thinking and stretch for new approaches to challenges and opportunities. This one gets a front seat in my leadership library."

DAVE PAZGAN
CEO, Kidokenetics

"When Allan asked me to review his new book, I hesitated. Will it have a new, compelling, and actionable message? Will it be well written? Will it contain personal and authentic stories? Will it guide and challenge people to achieve the seemingly impossible? My answer is yes! Read *Disruptable* and discover your inner disrupter!"

DAVE SUTTON
Chairman, TopRight Marketing
Author, *Marketing Interrupted*

"*Disruptable* is a must-read for anyone looking to unlock their full potential in business and beyond. Allan's perspectives and experiences will help shape your mindset and force you to step out of the ordinary to achieve maximum results."

BRIAN MATTINGLY
Founder and CEO, Welcomemat

"Allan is a compelling, credible storyteller. With keen insight and refreshing vulnerability, Allan shares practical wisdom from both his business successes and failures. For anyone who wants to lead effectively and impact others in today's world, *Disruptable* is a must-read book."

JUSTIN BREDEMAN
CEO, Soccer Shots

"In times of disruption, we can either surrender in defeat to the unforeseen change or let the chaos show us new opportunities. Allan takes this concept a step further and teaches us to wield disruption as a superpower for transforming our lives and surroundings toward an amazing future."

JOEL "THOR" NEEB
CEO, Afterburner
Author, *Survivor's Obligation*

"*Disruptable* will cause a dramatic shift in how you see yourself. If you want to upgrade your life in a significant way, break away from normal with the wisdom in *Disruptable*."

FRANK MILNER
CEO, Tudor Doctor

"A focused and intense guide full of plenty of powerful information for those of us that want to redefine ourselves and succeed in a challenging world."

CARLOS COSTE
Twelve-Time World Record Champion Freediver

"*Disruptable* offers a simple yet transformational process for continuous improvement, better leadership, and extraordinary growth. It is packed with insights on turning challenges into opportunities, embracing what makes us unique, and living with greater purpose. Throughout those meaningful principles Allan has woven in humorous and relatable stories such that every entrepreneur can benefit from the practice of intentional disruption in both their business and personal life."

MARK MOSES

CEO and Founding Partner, CEO Coaching International

"Allan has written a must-read for anyone who is on a quest to break away from normal and find the best version of themselves. Read this book, and learn from one of the best."

MARK SIEBERT

CEO, iFranchise Group

"Impactful, fast paced, and full of engaging stories, *Disruptable* shows how to disrupt yourself for continuous growth. A must-read if you're ready to break away from normal and become the best version of yourself."

DAVID PANTON

Cofounder, Navigation Capital Partners

"Allan's new book, *Disruptable,* is an authentic and genuine guide for current and future business leaders. Using personal and real-life examples, Allan exhibits his willingness to be vulnerable to help others avoid the mistakes and failures he experienced. Allan is a great teacher, mentor, and friend, as well as a sought-after leadership and business coach. He is always striving to learn and improve, both personally and professionally. We all have a lot to learn from his insights, methods, and tools, and I encourage every business leader looking to get to the next level to read *Disruptable* to glean some of his wisdom."

REBEKAH BARR
CEO, Allyon, Inc.

"*Disruptable* is the new *Blue Ocean Strategy* on steroids. If you are an individual contributor, a start-up entrepreneur, or a CEO running a multimillion-dollar company, we should all heed and embrace the words that Allan wrote to his son—'Never endeavor to be perfect. Instead, endeavor to be imperfect by constantly disrupting yourself.' We are all trying to move to the next level in our thoughts, careers, relationships, health, and happiness. *Disruptable* is our key to move to that next level, our highest level. Get ready for a transfiguration."

DR. KOFI SMITH
CEO, Keystone Management, LLC
Former President and CEO, Atlanta Airlines Terminal
Company at Hartsfield-Jackson Atlanta International Airport

"Allan's fearless approach to failure is wonderfully intertwined with lessons for both the reader's life and business. It's a truly honest must-read book for all entrepreneurs looking to share their vision and develop into authentic leaders. His disruptive entrepreneurial journey outlines a road map of how to succeed in today's fast-moving business climate."

RAFIQUE SYMONETTE
Managing Director, Bahamas Experience Tours

"Before *Disruptable*, I had not thought about disruption as a mindset and that I can choose to disrupt my life in a good way. Allan's experiences and stories allowed me to reflect on my personal quest for growth and to want to become more disruptable. As I read, I found myself looking forward to that next bit of wisdom."

JOHN MUNFORD
President, Riggins Company

"Buckle up and enjoy the ride as Allan's sheer determination to the ongoing process of becoming his best self takes you on his journey of epic failures and incredible successes."

JOHN R. DIJULIUS III
Best-Selling Author, *The Customer Service Revolution*

DISRUPTABLE

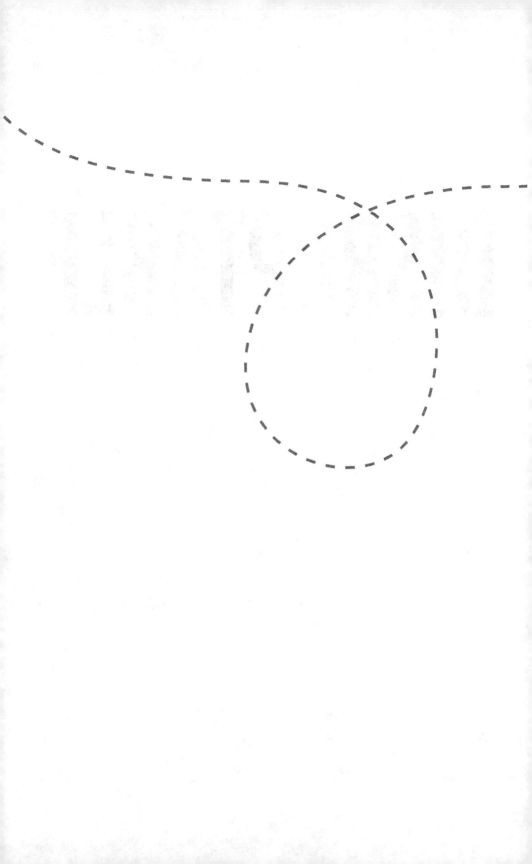

DISRUPTABLE

BREAK AWAY FROM
ORDINARY

ALLAN YOUNG
FOREWORD BY JACK DALY

ForbesBooks

Published by ForbesBooks, Charleston, South Carolina.
Member of Advantage Media Group.

ForbesBooks is a registered trademark, and the ForbesBooks colophon is a trademark of Forbes Media, LLC.

Printed in the United States of America.

10 9 8 7 6 5 4 3 2 1

ISBN: 978-1-94663-316-3
LCCN: 2022901617

Book design by Megan Elger.

This custom publication is intended to provide accurate information and the opinions of the author in regard to the subject matter covered. It is sold with the understanding that the publisher, Advantage|ForbesBooks, is not engaged in rendering legal, financial, or professional services of any kind. If legal advice or other expert assistance is required, the reader is advised to seek the services of a competent professional.

Since 1917, Forbes has remained steadfast in its mission to serve as the defining voice of entrepreneurial capitalism. ForbesBooks, launched in 2016 through a partnership with Advantage Media Group, furthers that aim by helping business and thought leaders bring their stories, passion, and knowledge to the forefront in custom books. Opinions expressed by ForbesBooks authors are their own. To be considered for publication, please visit **www.forbesbooks.com**.

To my son, Paige. Raising you made me a better man. Your curious nature and adventurous spirit continue to inspire me.

CONTENTS

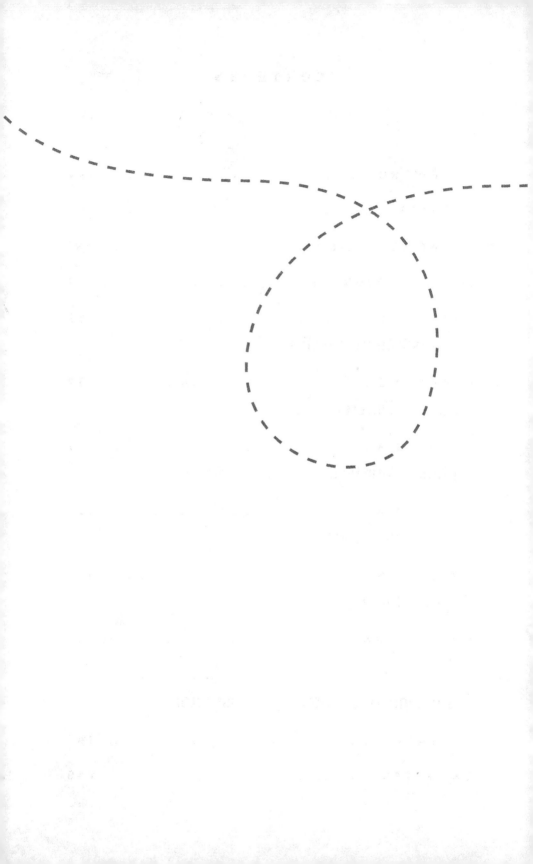

FOREWORD

Several years ago, I had the pleasure of meeting Allan Young in Atlanta prior to speaking to a group of entrepreneurs and business owners who were members of the Young Presidents' Organization. As we caught up on each other's personal and business histories, I marveled at the uncanny similarity in our lives. When Allan told me of his intent to write a book on his life lessons, I was keen to read it, as I knew it would bring real-life value to its readers. To be invited to pen the foreword is truly a privilege.

I regularly tout myself as a lifelong entrepreneur, having built my first company at age thirteen. I then learned that Allan had started fourteen businesses before entering high school! We laughed mightily at all the early life lessons learned from our successes and our failures. We share a special pride in having served in the US Army as officers, acquiring considerable leadership lessons that we positively leveraged in our business careers. Words such as self-reliant, resourceful, and resilient readily come to mind as the foundations for pursuing success in life, or as Allan put it: when confronted with something scary, run to it! It dawned on me that this must have been how I was able to take on marathons, Ironmans, skydiving, and bungee jumping, all of which were scary at the thought!

Over the ensuing years of our friendship, more shared behaviors came into play. Approaching life with a growth mindset is evidenced by our voracious love of reading or, as we call it, lifelong learning. So much of life's rich accomplishments have come as a by-product of a focus on goals. As Allan best says, it's the journey, not the destination, that's most important. All too often, as people age, they "settle" as if their life "is what it is." Allan reminds us with his drive that life can be both intentionally different and continuously improved. In effect, your life is by your own design.

As a coach to CEOs around the world, my favorite question is "Why?" Allan shares the same philosophy and takes it even further with "Why not?" His penchant for curiosity, creativity, and trying something different has resulted in countless tales of accomplishments and fun. Allan underscores that this approach to life is one where you are willing to fail. As he says, "Fail fast and learn from it."

I was glad Allan shared the value he placed on having a personal board of advisors. Bringing people you respect into your life as advisors can spare you great pains and accelerate your successes. Allan brings the concept of *grit* home loud and clear. While his accomplishments are extremely impressive, they are most valuable when viewed through his openly shared struggles and failures. Allan clearly shows the reader that we can set our course for life and make great things happen. He provides us a path for success through purposeful disruption by showing us that those who become Disruptable take intentional action both internally and externally. While I was furiously taking notes throughout the book, I was pleased to see he included a summary of key takeaways and action items at the close of each chapter. These provide the basis for designing your personal map for success.

Get ready to embrace your role as the disruptor!

Jack Daly
CEO coach, serial entrepreneur, Amazon best-selling author, and world-renowned professional speaker

PREFACE

Paige,

When you were born, I made a promise to myself that I would do everything possible to make you a better version of me. By that measure, I've done a fantastic job. I couldn't have imagined a better outcome. As you are starting your adventure into the Army, I know you are prepared to handle the challenges the military, and ultimately life, will throw at you.

Every parent has their shortfalls, and we raise our children through those insufficiencies. It's the child's responsibility to learn from and evolve beyond those shortfalls. There is little to learn from my successes, but there are many lessons in my most spectacular failures. Those lessons, accumulated over half of a lifetime, are my gift to you. The following are five lessons I'd like you to take on your life's journey:

    1. Life is a game. From the many games and adventures we've enjoyed together, you know winning a game requires that you see things that others do not. That clarity comes from vision. You find vision by simply being curious and asking questions that activate your imagination. Einstein said, "Imagination is everything. It's the preview to life's coming

attractions." Spend time imagining what winning looks like and *Why* you want that win. Sometimes your *Why* isn't easy to find. But that doesn't mean it's not there. Most people fall short of taking the necessary time to imagine their *Why* and create a clarity of vision that will propel them into meaningful wins. Take time to exercise and stretch your imagination and visualize what success looks like and *Why* you want it.

2. How you handle failure is what defines you. Failure is uncomfortable but less so if you fail fast. However, that doesn't mean giving up when life gets hard. Remember, you're always bigger than your failures. It's proof that you're pushing yourself to your limits. When you do that, you expand them. Repeatedly failing makes your potential limitless. Failure is never a person, only a point in time. In fact, at the peak point of failure, you are better than those around you experiencing success. Handling success is easy, and everyone can do it. Failure is hard, and if you step into it, the lessons you learn are a precious gift. You can harness your failures to continuously reinvent yourself and use them as a source of endless motivation.

3. Don't compare yourself with others. As one of your heroes, Teddy Roosevelt, said, "Comparison is the thief of all joy." Comparing yourself with others causes resentment. Instead, be the person you want to be. Choose to be *unordinary* by finding your different, embracing your fears, using your imagination to observe your impossible, and acting with intention to achieve it. Don't look for inspiration from others. Instead, be inspirational to others. The only person you should compare yourself with is the person you were yesterday.

4. Protect your mind. The people you hang around with will have a significant influence on how you think. Jim Rohn said, "You are the average of the five people you spend the most time with." When prioritizing friendships, ask three questions: Do they push me to be better? Do they hold me accountable? Do they encourage me to learn and grow? After you answer those three questions, ask yourself whether you should spend more or less time with them. Letting go of friends who fall into the latter category is tough, but remember, you're protecting your mind. You need to decide to be loved by these friends and remain the same person or become a better person at the cost of those friends.

5. Never endeavor to be perfect. Instead, endeavor to be imperfect by constantly disrupting yourself. The pursuit of perfection is a mirage that robs you of joy; don't spend your life chasing it. Lasting happiness does not come from money and success; it comes from doing the right thing, especially when it shows your imperfections. Embracing your imperfections opens the door to vulnerability. Exposing yourself to your vulnerabilities will allow you to truly know yourself and make deep and lasting connections with others. In the end, my vulnerability is my most important gift to you.

There are so many amazing and meaningful moments we've shared over the last eighteen years. Car camping, backpacking, swimming at 6 a.m. while grabbing Starbucks along the way and eating in the café afterward, fencing and sushi nights, shooting at the range, scuba and freediving, Wii Lego and Xbox adventures, TV shows we looked forward to watching together, trips to Haiti and the Dominican Republic to help others, New Zealand, Australia, China, the most amazing sunrise in Africa and the ride back to camp, and so many epic buddy days. Our bond is infinitely stronger than I could have ever hoped. When you were little, we'd say we were "buddies, boys, and pals." While we stopped saying those words as you got older, they became more true each day. Our relationship has grown to a level I could only imagine. While I'm very much your father and you are my son, you have become my brother.

You're not always going to make the right decisions or choices. The key is to exercise your best judgment and make them. Colin Powell, one of the greatest generals in modern history, said that every time you face a tough decision, you should have no less than 40 percent and no more than 70 percent of the information you need to make the decision. You'll be a great leader not by making the right decisions all the time but by making decisions when they need to be made. If you make the wrong decision and learn from it, that's a success, even though many around you will define it as a failure. That's OK. Just remember to fail fast and fail *forward*. When you do, know that I will *always* be there for you.

Love,
Dad

ACKNOWLEDGMENTS

Dad, I'll never fully comprehend how you balanced your job as a pastor of a church while raising two children. While everyone always received the best of you, you somehow made me feel like the most important person in the world. You are the most courageous, honest, and hardworking person I've known, and I am honored to be your son. The life lessons you taught me through your example were the ultimate gift. I respect and love you more than you will ever know.

Mom, your support for anything I wanted to be or do cannot be measured. You always nurtured my creative mind with so much love and support. I am so grateful for your constant inspiration to chase my dreams, regardless of how impossible they seem to be. Your constant encouragement combined with your enduring love is the single biggest reason for my success. Our bond and love are something only we can understand.

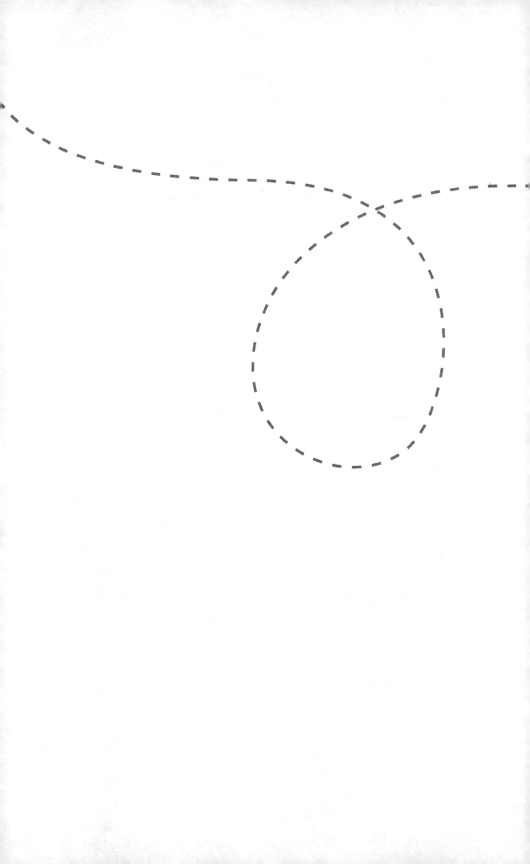

INTRODUCTION

When I was growing up, I was fortunate to have parents who encouraged me to question everything. They celebrated imagination and curiosity. They constantly supported me and always told me I could be and do anything I wanted. They supported my visions of what I wanted to do and who I wanted to become. I embraced that support, and throughout my childhood, that support led to incredible successes and magnificent failures.

My first memorable *Why* question came when I was five years old. There were over ten kids in the neighborhood, and we were always playing outside, exploring the woods, shooting bottle rockets at one another, and playing hide-and-go-seek. During one of those moments, Mr. Ferguson asked me to help him pull weeds out of his garden. He was always super nice to me and was always giving vegetables from his garden to my mom. So it was an easy "sure" from me.

When I was done, he gave me $5. I couldn't believe it. That was a ton of money back then, especially at that age. I had no idea you could make money by helping people out. It was very unexpected, especially since I didn't ask for it. My theory was simple: if you helped people out with no expectation of getting something out of it, they would want to give you something in return.

I was curious if this theory was true. I immediately rounded up all the kids and told them about my idea. I called it the Work Club. Yeah, not the most original name, but we were always looking for something new to try, especially if it didn't result in a bottle rocket or BB gun aimed at your face. I made my vision for the group clear: if we worked hard and fast, we could accomplish more jobs than the day before. It was a game to see how much we could get done. It was no different from the other games we played, but this one had the most measurable and satisfying results. We could look back on that yard and see the results of our efforts. Everyone was on board.

We began our new venture immediately. I'd knock on a neighbor's door and ask if there were any outside chores they wanted us to do. They'd look at the group of smiling and motivated kids behind me, and they'd give us a task like pulling weeds (that was my go-to suggestion), raking leaves, or clearing out their garage. They'd usually ask how much, and I'd tell them it was what our Work Club did, and they didn't have to pay us.

My theory turned out to be correct. If you don't ask for anything in return for doing work (and you're a kid), you will get paid handsomely. Sometimes one of the kids would get lazy, lax, or disinterested. Without much effort on my part, the rest of the kids would get on them and tell them they either needed to work as hard as them to accomplish our task or go home. In those days, leaving whatever the group was doing resulted in a brutal punishment: boredom. There wasn't an Instagram feed, Snapchat, or Xbox world to fall back on. Most kids stepped up their game to avoid it. Occasionally, the group would banish a kid from the Work Club for repeatedly violating our unstated culture without me having to say a word. I just focused on reminding them that if we finished this job, we could move on to the next one I found just a few houses over.

Things were going fabulously. Then one day my parents came into my room as I was organizing my money into stacks of $1s, $5s, $10s, and $20s. My dad looked at me and asked me where I got the stacks of cash, and I told him excitedly about the Work Club and how amazing it was. We were having fun, *and* I was making lots of money.

Then came his next question: "How much are you paying the other kids?" At first, his question was a bit of a surprise. Why would I need to pay them? They were happy to work for free. All was good. I smiled proudly and said, "Nothing! They're happy to do it for free!" I was proud of my answer for about three seconds until I read his expression. There was instant confusion on my part. Suddenly, my idea that seemed so perfect for everyone involved didn't seem so perfect. I sheepishly tried to explain myself. "Dad, they all like doing it (which was true), and I even give them orange Tic Tacs while they're doing the work." The hole was getting deeper. He was uncovering the truth and wasn't impressed. Not only was I not doing any work and taking all the money, but I was also walking around dropping Tic Tacs into their mouths while they were working. (To be fair, handing them out to them while they had rakes, weeds, or garage junk in their hands would have been unsanitary.)

The Work Club was officially out of business. I felt incredibly guilty after that interaction with my dad. If you've never had a Baptist minister look at you while you're trying to explain your way out of a bad idea, you've never fully lived. I quickly got on my bike and rode to the small store near my house that sold both candy (including orange Tic Tacs) and cowboy-style cap guns. I cleaned them out of stock and distributed the spoils to everyone in the Work Club. Luckily, they were ecstatic with the outcome. They knew I was keeping the money and just wanted to be in the club (probably because I'd kick people out if they didn't work hard enough). Bonusing out all the money in the form of the real currency at our age brought smiles to their faces. I was the hero of the moment, but I didn't feel like one.

The reason I told you that embarrassing story is simple. Having a curious mind and a strong imagination can lead to a powerful vision that people want to follow. A powerful vision will always lead to both success and failure. Sometimes the failure is masked as outward success. The failure can lead to learning and growth, which is the biggest success if you are introspective, learn, and adjust. I didn't learn anything from the success of making that money, but I learned a ton from that difficult conversation with my dad and the painful introspection that followed. It was the first of many "failures that looked like wins" when I was a kid. I started fourteen businesses before I was in high school. Each one failed at some point for a variety of reasons, and I learned painful but critical lessons from each.

A few years later, while most kids in the neighborhood had a treehouse, I wanted mine to be the biggest and best treehouse. It needed to be incredible. I had a vision of what it would look like. When my dad saw me unsuccessfully (and unsafely) trying to build this monstrosity, he decided to step in, and since he was great working with wood, it turned out amazing. *Everyone* wanted to hang out in my treehouse. As large as it was, there wasn't room enough for everyone. If I picked who could come up, it resulted in those not chosen being upset. My solution was simple. I charged five cents for an hour in the treehouse. That didn't work. Still too much demand for the available space. I experimented with my pricing model. It turned out twenty-five cents for a half an hour in the treehouse was

> Having a curious mind and a strong imagination can lead to a powerful vision that people want to follow.

the sweet spot. Things in the new venture were perfect … for about a week.

As soon as my parents began getting calls from other parents who were upset that instead of playing in their own treehouses, their kids were *paying* to hang out in mine, I was forced out of business. Since the demand was still there, I figured out a different approach. I designated three team captains, and they did a schoolyard pick for their teams. Each had a schedule of when they could use the treehouse. Since it was mine, I got to participate with any of the teams whenever I wanted. Problem solved, and there went another business down the drain.

The lesson I learned from that experience was different from the one I would learn later in life. At the time, I didn't think it was fair that I couldn't charge money, but when I adjusted to a no-fee structure, I still had fun. As I look back on it, I created something that all great companies do at their core: they create an amazing experience and charge for it. I was too young at the time to understand that premise. I was stuck in a world that didn't allow for entrepreneurial creation. Of course, those same parents would pay out huge sums of money to take their kids to theme parks, but they weren't OK with my younger version of that. It was fine to sell lemonade but not experiences.

I was not deterred. Within a few months, I identified another opportunity. Since my dad was a Baptist minister, he had one of the first cassette tape recorders in the neighborhood. Remember the kind that was like a flattened brick powered with *D* batteries, and you pressed play and record at the same time to record something? Yep, I had unfettered access to it when my dad wasn't looking. The neighborhood kids were fascinated by it. They had never been able to record their own voices and listen to them played back. I let them record anything they wanted to say for thirty seconds for *free*. If they wanted to hear it played back, the price was ten cents per playback.

Based on all the bad words they recorded, they all wanted to hear it played back over and over (think TikTok and Spotify having a baby that's a cassette tape). Win-win, right? Not really. Again, with that kind of outflow of cash in the neighborhood, someone was bound to notice. And once again, my business was shut down by forces more powerful than I am. Luckily, no parents got access to that cassette tape.

From there, I created a pine cone air freshener manufacturing and retail sales company in the woods behind my house. Sales were good, but I found the workforce lazy and difficult to motivate. I created a neighborhood newspaper where I enlisted all the kids to become reporters. The stories were handwritten multiple times on triplicate paper and then sorted and stapled together to be distributed and sold by those who lacked writing skills. Later, I got my own commercial crabbing license, so I could sell crabs to tourists on Colonial Beach, where we spent every summer. It was a solo venture with my younger friend Johnny King serving as my helpful apprentice. I found it refreshing having just one employee. I started new businesses about every year—some failed quickly, others thrived briefly, and several barely passed the test of mediocrity.

By the time I was in high school, I had fourteen businesses under my belt and even more failures and lessons learned. My parents supported my insane curiosity to try, fail, and learn from as many things as possible. At that point in my life, I thought of failure as an experience rather than a negative event. I learned that if you're going to fail, it's best to fail fast. Getting a chance to move on to something new and challenging was exciting and its own reward. Some lessons were immediate (don't get your friends to work for free), and others came later in life after reflection. My definition of failure wasn't a bad one, until high school.

Being different was encouraged, at least by my parents. Their support, especially when I failed or did something wrong, allowed me to learn from those failures. But in adolescence, something changes for all of us. There are outside pressures that encourage us to become normal, "ordinary." In fact, you're encouraged to become extraordinary. The pressure to normalize is intense, and most of us are drawn into it. For someone who thrived on my differences growing up, I found myself developing a desire to fit in, to be normal, in high school. I did try. I joined groups and tried not to stand out. It turned out there wasn't a bucket for creative entrepreneurs in high school, and I didn't fit into one of the standard roles of jock, nerd, popular, or skater dude.

High school is where the real discussion of what you're going to be when you grow up starts. Like the buckets for high school groups, there were finite options for careers. When I told my guidance counselor that I wanted to start my own business, her response was a slight chuckle as she told me, "You need to go to college, get a job at a good company, and maybe later in life you can look into that." It also didn't help that I wasn't a great student. I was a solid C– student because I didn't find anything I was passionate about in high school, and I wasn't good at being a generalist ... someone who is above average at everything. I loved leading and found I could do that quickly by starting companies. Those concepts weren't encouraged in high school in the 1980s. An entrepreneur in the '80s was your crazy uncle who started businesses and lost all his money several times. Not cool.

In my junior year, I decided to join a club. After a careful analysis of my options, I joined the Teenage Republicans because it had the second-largest number of cute girls. The French Club had the most, but since they spoke only French at their meetings, that one was out.

(I got a D– in French.) If I was going to be a joiner, this club seemed like the best choice. Things went well that year. It was fun because of the cute girls, and I even got a girlfriend for a few weeks out of the deal. (Three weeks was a solid number back then.) In case you're wondering, based on the demographics of my hometown, there wasn't a thriving Young Democrats Club at my high school.

At the beginning of my senior year, I showed up to the first Teenage Republican meeting, and only three other people showed up. Where were all the cool people and cute girls? As it turned out, many of the members the previous year had been seniors, and the rest didn't show up because they knew the majority had graduated. The teacher in charge of the club announced we needed to pick officers for the club. With lightning speed, I volunteered to be the president, which didn't come close to matching the reactions (if there were going to be any) of the other three. I quickly started assigning the other roles (vice president, secretary, and treasurer), and now we were in business.

The next day, I created my uniform: a navy blazer and tie with khaki pants, and I replaced my backpack with a briefcase. For the rest of my senior year, I wore that uniform ... to public school. Over the next few months, I recruited over one hundred members to the club with promises of my vision. We'd raise enough money to take the entire club to Washington, DC, for a weekend trip. A club going on a weekend field trip to another city was unprecedented. I made the promise with both a clear vision and a plan. We'd raise money with an aluminum can drive to fund and promote a citywide fundraising dance where all the high schools in the area were invited (another unprecedented move).

I was passionate about making this succeed. We put a large trash can that was marked "Cans Only" next to the Coke vending machine at our school. While successful in collecting cans for recycling (you got money for turning in aluminum cans at the recycling plant back then), we weren't raising enough funds for the dance that needed deposits for the large banquet hall, DJ, lights, and caterer. I sprang into action by attending all the unsanctioned parties each weekend. Because I was the president of the club that almost everyone joined, I was invited to these parties, albeit with a second-class social status. I showed up and spent the entire time walking around with a black trash bag, picking up empty beer cans, and asking people if they were done with the beer can next to them.

Over several months, I collected enough cans to make the deposits for the dance. Everyone in the group promoted the dance, and we sold over 350 tickets to people from all five local high schools. It raised enough money for everyone in the club who wanted to go on the trip to stay in a four-star hotel (a far cry from most of our experience vacationing and staying in poorly maintained motels on our summer vacations with our parents). We spent the weekend touring the monuments and museums. Everyone had a blast, and it was the talk of the school for the next few weeks.

While that venture was a success, I was typecast my senior year as the guy in the coat and tie that collected empty beer cans instead of drinking them. (I found that drinking beer clouded my ability to focus and perform that task with excellence.) It was another success that resulted in a failure. Later in life, I realized the failures that taught me success were found in understanding my different, not trying to be ordinary, and authentically pursuing a vision, even at the expense of not fitting in.

In adolescence, we are pressured to believe being different, making mistakes, and failing is bad. In high school, I was taught to fit in, get good grades, and try to be good at everything. The lesson they were trying to teach was clear: the best version of ourselves is not a reflection of our possibilities but a reflection of the average of everyone else around us. It was comparison without context.

When we compare ourselves with everyone around us, we're really comparing ourselves with the average of everyone around us. The ordinary. Of course, we're all encouraged to become extraordinary. It seems logical, but we lose sight of who we are and what we're capable of becoming. We lose sight of what's possible, the radical options of our possibilities. My lesson from those experiences was the beginning of what became clear later in life: by pursuing the unordinary and continually and intentionally disrupting myself, I could create radically better versions of myself. That goal of continuous, radical improvement became my definition of success. Embracing that discomfort of change became my mantra. Multiple disrupted versions of myself have at times determined that I'm not a Republican (or Democrat), I only wear a coat and tie to funerals, and my attention to detail on recycling cans is slightly above par. Those things are no longer important to me, but they are a part of my story of self-disruption. I wouldn't give up any of those experiences because I learned something from each of them.

When you think disruption, do you envision someone who is fighting against the grain to change themselves? Someone who will challenge their beliefs and even traditions? When you disrupt yourself, when disruption is *intentionally focused on something bigger than who you are currently,* incredible things happen. Just look at Nikola Tesla, Abraham Lincoln, Martin Luther King Jr., Ruth Bader Ginsburg, Marie Curie, and Albert Einstein. These visionaries turned industries and govern-

Don't try to be a better version of yourself—become an unrecognizable version of yourself.

ments on their heads and changed how we communicate, consume, and think, and they didn't do it only for themselves. They had a vision and passion for solving problems and making positive change for everyone. They took risks, endured massive doses of failure, and evolved not only their ideas but also themselves.

They all shared one thing in common: they were all Disruptable. They all changed themselves more than they asked others to change. They did it by poking holes in problems that no one else had the foresight to solve. They poked, they looked to the future, they took risks, they planned, and they solved. They failed. They understood that being unordinary would unlock their potential.

That's what *intentional* disruption looks like—strategically finding ways to make positive, explosive change to yourself. Don't try to be a *better* version of yourself—become an unrecognizable version of yourself. My goal is to be an *unrecognizable* version of myself every five years. That can't happen without a willingness to be vulnerable enough to fail as often as necessary. Failure is growth. What's your appetite for it?

When I graduated high school, while I was accepted into a few mediocre colleges, I was self-aware enough to know I wouldn't last a semester at those schools. I lacked self-discipline (easy to do when you're a creative person with twenty ideas a day). I elected to do a post-graduate year at Hargrave Military Academy in Chatham, Virginia. It was basically a thirteenth grade. I managed to secure a congressional appointment to West Point my senior year. My grades weren't even close to meeting West Point standards, but my SATs were surprisingly high. West Point wrote back to me and said that if I raised my GPA while attending this military boarding school, I would be accepted.

I'd always been attracted to the Army and knew that if I went to Hargrave, I would get my grades up and get into West Point. I had no idea that year and my subsequent military training would further introduce me to *intentional* disruption.

People who first learn how to disrupt themselves and then learn how to disrupt others are the people who change the world. This change doesn't have to happen on a large stage, and it doesn't have to be done by a Jobs or a Bezos or a Musk. The world you change can be your neighborhood, your workplace, or your family. Intentional disruption is for everyone. A leader can disrupt herself and then show those she leads a way to get results by creating a radically different company culture. A call center agent can disrupt themselves and lead their peers by influencing them through an example of continuous growth. I've seen this type of disruption happen more times than I can count, and every time it's awe inspiring. Anyone who is willing to disrupt themselves can be a radical disruptor, and it all starts with a willingness to become Disruptable.

After spending five years learning how to disrupt myself as an Army officer stationed at Schofield Barracks, Hawaii, I applied my obsessive interest in problem-solving back into business. In 2001, I launched my first business as an adult, Total Home Connections. It was a home automation business that was Geek Squad before Geek Squad existed. I sold that business two years later after realizing that while I made lots of money, I wasn't changing anyone's lives for the better. Sure, a fully automated home is cool, but selling more stuff to people who already have tons of stuff didn't make a meaningful difference for me.

In 2003, I started a whole-house air purification company that used carbon-based air filters to remove organic compounds and bacteria from the air and UV lights that killed any viruses that passed through it. That was a fantastic business. It had a major impact on people's lives, especially those suffering from allergies, asthma, and COPD. It was one of my most successful and painful failures. Just after my first year of starting that business, I received a note from the Army reminding me that I was still in the Reserves, and I was to report to a beach again. However, this beach had no water. I had just over six months to get ready for my deployment to the Middle East. I knew that while my business was successful, I couldn't run it from over seven thousand miles away, and I immediately put it up for sale.

There was a lot of interest in my rapidly growing business. However, I had brought in most of the sales personally, and my other salespeople hadn't performed as well. We also experienced high turnover as I learned to both hire and lead a home improvement labor force. While the buyer didn't give me the money up front, we agreed to an earn-out. An earn-out is a payment for the business based on the future success of the company. The lucrative earn-out was to begin six months after they took over the business. I received notice two months into my deployment that the company had failed.

I had put almost all my time and energy into that business. I worked sixteen-hour days Monday through Saturday with a shorter eight-hour day on Sunday to catch up on things when it was quiet. I thought that's what you needed to do to be successful as an entrepreneur in the adult world. Of course, that's what we're all told. But here's the thing, when you spend that much time propping up your business every day, you *are* the business. Witnessing the failure of something that I had built with so much time, energy, and passion hurt deeply. The pit in my stomach lasted a couple of years until I figured out how to learn from it.

Adding to that feeling was the public failure of my business. I quickly learned that in the adult world, public failure felt different than when I was a kid. Entrepreneurial failures are incredibly public.

If you don't get into law school, no one needs to know. If you get fired from a job, you can explain to everyone that you quit to find something better. But when your business fails, everyone knows it, especially, thanks to the internet, in an increasingly connected society. I had to rethink my definition of failure in this setting. While those close to you understand the whole story, to everyone else, there is only one story: you failed.

When I returned from my deployment, I found a new business. In 2005, I started consulting with Shelf Conversions, a Richmond-based company owned by a mother-and-son team that wanted to franchise. Within a year, I became a partner and received a percentage of ownership in the company for my efforts and results. A year later, I bought the business from them with the help of angel investors. In the fall of 2008, with the economy quickly deteriorating into a major recession, I launched ShelfGenie Franchise Systems. Fear, uncertainty, and doubt were the emotions anyone owning a business was feeling during that time. It seemed failure was always lurking around the corner.

As it turned out, it was a great time to launch a franchise. Since we launched in the recession, it was the only world we knew. We built the company in that environment, sold a ton of franchises, and were an *Entrepreneur 500* company in 2009 and an *Inc. 500* company in 2010. Today ShelfGenie has over two hundred locations in the United States and Canada.

The only reason for my success in that business was my failure in my air purification company. The one that did so well when I was working sixteen hours a day and fell apart when I left it. The lesson I learned from that business as an entrepreneur was simple: don't be the business. From the beginning with ShelfGenie, I built a great team. What was my close rate when I ran appointments? Zero percent, because I never ran an appointment. I found people better than me at selling. Everything from sales, marketing, finance to operations, I focused on one thing: find people better than me to do the work. I still knew every inch of that business, but I wasn't the business. My message to prospective franchisees when they'd come to our office for a Discovery Day to decide if they wanted to buy a franchise was simple: everything they saw in the business from the support systems, our customer support call center, sales training to marketing support we offered had been built on my past failures.

Traditionally, the franchisor gives the franchisees tremendous support at the beginning and then little support as they move through the life cycle of their business. For franchisees, this can be difficult. They pay a large sum to get the franchise, and then it becomes a "what have you done for me lately" mentality as they continue to pay for royalties and support. We chose to build a franchise model that did everything for our franchisees—customer support, media, marketing, ordering, and manufacturing—so they could focus on growing their business instead of working in their business. That was the secret to ShelfGenie's success, and it was all based on past failures.

I continued to build on the franchise model I created for ShelfGenie to founding Outback GutterVac, a high-tech gutter cleaning company; G.O. Logistics, a wholesale logistics company servicing each of our companies; Freedom Suite Services, a marketing and sales center firm; and acquiring Cabinet Component Innovations, a technology-driven manufacturer of cabinet components. Those moves, which most around me considered both radical and risky, resulted in the combination of those businesses and their franchise companies generating over $50 million in annual revenues. A great scoreboard of success that was built on countless failures, many of which I've outlined in this book.

In *Disruptable*, I will show you how to change your mindset so that you can positively disrupt yourself and your world. You will learn the following:

- How to rediscover and embrace what makes you different from others

- How to confront your fears and use them to grow

- How to observe the impossible to make changes in yourself that you didn't think were possible

- How to act intentionally to set yourself up for whatever greatness you want to achieve

Because I am an entrepreneur, many of the stories in *Disruptable* are about how leaders, friends, and I have disrupted ourselves first and how that resulted in radical change for not only ourselves but also for the people around us and our industries. However, intentional disruption is for everyone who wants to find their impossible self. Once you disrupt yourself, you'll find a better you. Today I don't even recognize the person I was five, ten, or fifteen years ago. By disrupting myself, I've continued to challenge my beliefs mentally, physically, and spiritually. Always remember failure *is* an option. You don't go looking for it, but it will find you. When it does, embrace it, fail fast, and learn from it. I can't think of a time I learned anything valuable from success, but every time I've failed, I've grown both personally and professionally.

The challenges you face will create opportunities *if* you can disrupt yourself. Intentional disruption is a mindset. Like any mindset, it can be learned. The Disruptable mindset can be learned through mastering the four steps in this book. In any military training I ever did or led, the goal was to create a more miserable, challenging environment than the one you're planning to face. That's a challenging training focus, and it's the same focus you need to become Disruptable. Disrupt yourself more than anyone that you ask to follow you. This process is not linear and can be applied to any situation you face in life. Get ahead of the curve and proactively disrupt yourself radically to create seemingly impossible change and countless opportunities for others.

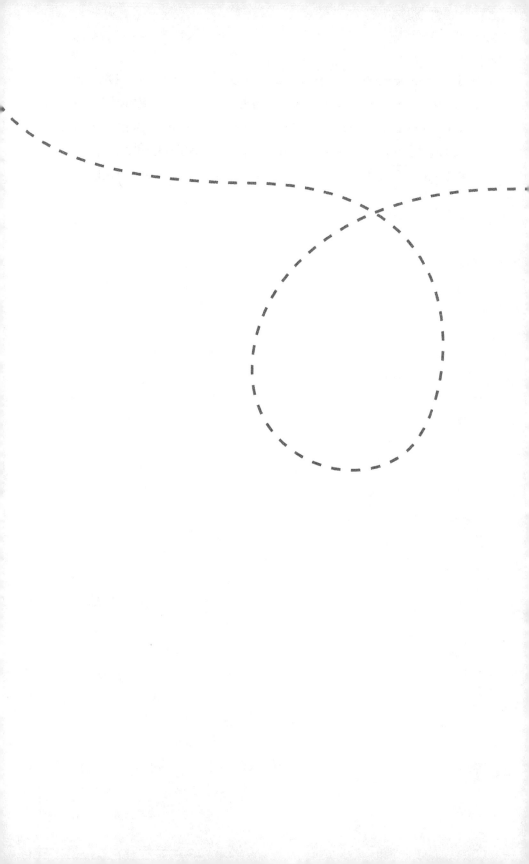

CHAPTER 1

What Is Intentional Disruption?

*The chief task in life is simply this: to identify and separate matters
so that I can say clearly to myself which are externals not under
my control and which have to do with the choices I actually control.
Where then do I look for good and evil? Not to uncontrollable
externals, but within myself to the choices that are my own.*
—EPICTETUS, *DISCOURSES*

STATEMENTS OF AN INTENTIONAL DISRUPTOR

Each chapter features a different quiz where you can rate your
path toward intentional disruption. On a scale of 1–5, with 1 being
the least, rate your relatability to the following statements:

_____ I influence others.

_____ I achieve things others think are impossible.

_____ I don't recognize myself from five years ago.

_____ I aggressively pursue continual improvement.

Are you ready to be a disruptor?

One of the reasons military schools are so successful in helping young men and women who are struggling is that they strip them of themselves. At the age of eighteen, I walked into Hargrave Military Academy, and all preconceived notions of myself disappeared. I wore a gray uniform like everyone else. I studied for two hours every night with my door open like everyone else. I lived in a room with a window on the door and no lock like everyone else, and like everyone else, I followed orders. Although I voluntarily went to Hargrave for a year after high school in the hopes of getting good enough grades to get into West Point, I had no idea how significantly Hargrave would change my life.

When something is taken from you, it's all you think about. Hargrave took my individuality. For an entire year, I thought about the person I had been and the person I wanted to be. I had started life as a disruptor—I ran businesses out of treehouses and crab boats—and in high school, I resisted the push toward the status quo—to fit in.

At Hargrave, I spent hours reflecting on how I'd gravitated away from being comfortable with myself to blending into the status quo. When everyone is the same, you genuinely look for how you're different as an individual. Because of the introspection that Hargrave forced upon me, I learned to intentionally disrupt myself, and I'm forever grateful for that miserable experience.

Intentional Disruption Defined

Being Disruptable is a process of understanding who you are and embracing your fears to unlock creativity and imagination for long-term personal growth. Intentional disruption is a process that requires you to disrupt yourself before you effect change in others. It's like the flight attendant's request that, in case of an emergency, you put your oxygen mask on first before helping others. If you don't help yourself first, how are you going to help anyone else? If you practice intentional self-disruption, you won't need to worry about creating external disruption because it will occur naturally and sometimes magically.

In *Disruptable*, I will show you how to go through the disruption process internally first so you can help others later. I will show you how to make yourself vulnerable, face your fears, get out of your comfort zone, question everything you believe, have courage that only comes through fear, see new opportunities, and embrace what's considered impossible. It is a circular rather than a linear process, and you may feel compelled to skip certain chapters and return to them later. You may feel like you've mastered facing your fears but need help finding your different. Or you know what makes you different, but you struggle to embrace curiosity. Wherever you are on your path to intentional disruption, the tips and stories in *Disruptable* will guide you toward making long-lasting, positive change.

What Are the Characteristics of an Intentional Disruptor?

Intentional disruption isn't limited to introverts or extroverts, CEOs or entry-level positions, men or women, children or adults. It's accessible to anyone willing to do the hard work that introspection demands. Not only are intentional disruptors introspective, but they also

- focus on solutions rather than obstacles,

- create purpose,

- lead by influence rather than control, and

- have a growth mindset.

PRACTICE INTROSPECTION

Intentional disruptors never shy away from the challenges presented by introspection. When I was at Hargrave and was stripped of my high school identity, I had no choice but to look at myself. I didn't like what I saw. I saw a person who was slowly letting go of their creativity. I saw a person who felt the pressures of conformity and who lost their entrepreneurial spirit. The whole idea of being someone that you think others want you to be is pervasive in high school. For many high school students, the game becomes how to make the fewest mistakes and fit in. Unfortunately, that pressure is the training grounds for a life of more of the same.

But at Hargrave, I wasn't given that option. Instead, I was forced to look in the mirror. It was painful to look at myself. I had thought that I could choose any adventure, but the more reflective I became, the more I realized that the options for adventures given to me were severely limited. It's like those adventure books that let you pick what comes next. I used to love getting those at the book fair in elementary school. I loved them because they gave you choices. I was beginning to figure out that in those books and in life, while you have some influence on the outcome, someone else defines those choices and even the possible outcomes.

I was beginning to figure this out at Hargrave because the lifestyle didn't allow any external choices. Our clothes and routine were the same. This homogeny almost created a meditative environment because there was nothing to look at or be distracted by. It was a miserable experience, and all I wanted to do was go home. I desperately wanted to return to what I knew and where I was comfortable.

Going back to Hargrave after Christmas break was hard. I knew I didn't have to return. It was always my choice. I could just go to college. Remembering that it was a choice was the defining moment for me. More importantly, this was why I made the choice to go to Hargrave in the first place. I was there to create structure and build discipline within myself because I knew I wasn't disciplined enough to attain the future I envisioned for myself. I chose to return to Hargrave and embrace the opportunity to rebuild myself: I began to make the necessary changes from within.

Although my introspection was painful, it allowed me to take a few steps back to determine how I wanted to move forward. From that experience, I stopped spinning my wheels and started moving down the path that was right for me. I understood why I never quite felt like I fit into any of the groups that I joined in high school—none of them had been right for the real me. At Hargrave, I was able to establish my unique path forward by examining my passion and potential to create my own vision for my life. That process instilled a confidence in me that set me up for the rest of my life.

Introspection is not a one-and-done proposition. Yes, my introspection at Hargrave established a foundation to move forward from, but I continue to actively examine my life and my true self. I think fear is one of my big motivators that leads to introspection. Whenever something frightens me, I want to go do it. I've learned from experience that when you do scary things, you learn a lot about yourself, you learn significant life lessons, and you grow.

One of the things I like about freediving, paragliding, skydiving, and other fear-inducing experiences is they provide an environment where you can observe yourself. You're navigating a situation in which your brain is screaming that what you are doing is irrational. You quiet that scream by learning how to become comfortable with both physical and emotional discomfort. Mental, and sometimes physical, pain is required to overcome that discomfort. When you intentionally put yourself in uncomfortable situations, your brain begins to get used to the feeling and learns to deal with it. Learning to get comfortable being uncomfortable definitely comes in handy when facing other fears, especially ones that don't involve a physical threat.

FOCUS ON SOLUTIONS RATHER THAN OBSTACLES

In the Army, we were taught to assess obstacles when we came across them. Sometimes the best course of action is to go around the obstacle. Other times it's to breach the obstacle. Think about a very high wall you come across in your path while conducting a mission. It's a problem, so you focus on it. You have some options: breach (destroy part of it) it or go over it. Next, you begin thinking about the resources needed to climb over or destroy it. Pretty logical stuff for a mission-oriented military leader. However, if you take a step back, other options start to emerge. Perhaps digging a hole under it may be simple compared with the first options. You can also take time to assess how wide the wall is. Walls don't go forever, and sometimes the solution is taking a different path from the one you planned and walking around the obstacle.

> When you intentionally put yourself in uncomfortable situations, your brain begins to get used to the feeling and learns to deal with it.

When you intently focus on obstacles, they get in your way. But, on the other hand, if you observe them as a potential to adjust and change course, they're nothing more than an excuse to get creative.

CREATE PURPOSE

Intentional disruption always starts with a problem. The disruptor finds a need that no one else addresses or something poorly done and does something to change it. That change is how we create purpose.

Creating purpose is precisely what Dr. Bob Simon did when he founded International Medical Corps in 1984. Nancy Aossey, IMC's president and CEO, talks about the why and how of the organization's almost forty years of intentional disruption in its mission to help the most vulnerable populations in remote areas of the world.

In the early years of IMC, most humanitarian organizations could only work in certain parts of the world because it was deemed too dangerous to reach people in certain areas. As a result, there were multitudes of people who were in need of support or training or humanitarian assistance living in regions that were too remote to safely access. Our whole premise was to disrupt that paradigm and ask the question why. Why can't we reach people in remote Afghanistan? Why can't we train people in their own country? How do we solve for the need? The disruptive nature, the risk-taking, the idea that we were going to focus on looking at where the gaps were and solve for the gaps is what personally drew me to the organization.

One of our first humanitarian efforts was an operation in Soviet-occupied Afghanistan. When the Soviet Union invaded, they imprisoned, exiled, or killed the doctors and nurses so that the Afghan people would be unable to access healthcare. Afghans were dying by the thousands and needed aid, but it was incredibly dangerous to work inside the country, so humanitarian organizations set up medical care on the border. But the challenge was that the Afghan people had to travel by foot, over mountainous terrain, to reach the aid at the border. Many people didn't survive the trek, and those that did landed in refugee camps with no option to safely return home. At IMC,

25

we determined our purpose was to get healthcare to the people inside the country, so they wouldn't have to travel to the border or become refugees for the rest of their lives. We solved for all the obstacles, and in the end, we set up a medic-training program, and we trained Afghans to be medics. Those who went through our nine-month intensive training program treated 85–90 percent of all the injuries and diseases that occurred. We assessed the obstacles, the limitations, and the risks. We then created a formula and approach that worked for the Afghan people and maintained the highest level of safety possible for our humanitarian workers.

We have since developed and executed hundreds of humanitarian operations throughout the world. Every operation is drastically different, and this continuous level of disruption requires us to constantly orient, reassess, create a new path, and make adjustments every day. We do this through what we call after-action reviews, similar to those used in the military. We utilize these action reviews as close to real-time as possible to course correct and pivot quickly. It's challenging to do when you're in the middle of an emergency's chaos. Still, it's also incredibly valuable to do in the heat of the moment because you're able to make a necessary adjustment in real-time that can change the operation's level of success.

The fear of physical harm, and even death, is a daily reality for the IMC workers and the people they serve. On the topic of overcoming this fear, this is what Nancy had to say:

This was many years ago, but I still remember it so clearly today. I asked one of the Afghan women who completed our training program, "How do you do it? You've lost so much. There's so much uncertainty in your life. There's so much danger and risk to you personally. How do you keep going?"

She told me that IMC gave her hope. "When I found a path to help my people, I got my life back. I got hope. And I felt there's nothing in the world I can't face now."

I remember thinking that is the essence of what drives our work. For me, and I know for many of my comrades, focusing on the work itself and the bigger purpose is a way to channel that fear. It is the mindset that what I'm doing gives my life meaning, gives my life purpose, and whatever the risk and whatever the danger is, I'm going to face it because I'm working on something bigger than myself.

Intentional disruptors seek to understand why things aren't being done and why specific problems aren't being solved. Generally, the answer to both is fear. Most people fear doing the hard, radical thing that will solve the problem. Intentional disruptors have learned the ability to see through the darkness of their fear. They are masters of observation and creativity and use that skill to find unique solutions to problems.

LEAD BY INFLUENCE RATHER THAN CONTROL

Intentional disruptors know that influence trumps control all day long. Through influence, they get those around them to buy into a bigger dream. They don't use the power of position to get things done. They don't have to be in a leadership position. Instead, they focus on achieving a common goal that makes the pie bigger versus taking a bigger slice of the pie. They do it through collaboration and interaction rather than coercion. They encourage vigorous debate from their teams before making a decision.

The military is a great case study on how leaders can choose influence over control. The people you lead are under lawful order to comply with your orders. If they don't, they are punished under the uniform code of military justice and can be confined to their quarters, docked pay, reduced in rank, and imprisoned. Pretty harsh stuff. There is no need for influence leadership because leadership by control is embedded, but that doesn't mean it is more effective. My experience demonstrated that influence leadership is far more effective than leadership through control.

I went to my Army officer training the summer after my junior year. During the training, you're constantly being evaluated. Everyone rotates leadership positions, so one day you're a squad leader, another day you're the platoon leader, and the next day you're just a regular member of the squad. After six weeks of evaluation in a barracks environment and field training leading missions, you receive your evaluation. You receive an overall score on a scale of 1–5. At that time, to score a 5, you needed to show that you could scream and yell at your soldiers when you were in command. It was modeling the stereotypical military approach that you see in movies. I didn't do that. Instead, I used influence, and my team achieved all the objectives on our missions. No yelling and screaming. No forceful "talks" that were meant to intimidate. When I graduated, I received a 4.

My tactical officer's feedback was that I wasn't forceful enough and didn't "motivate" enough when leading my squad. I questioned his definition of motivation—not my best decision. I was put into a position of parade rest (hands behind your back, feet spread apart while staring straight forward and not making eye contact) while I received a ten-minute "motivating" talk designed to ensure I understood his point of view. The Army calls these talks significant emotional events. That significant emotional event only reinforced my belief that he was wrong. Using better judgment, I responded, "Yes, sir!" and walked away, determined to never lead that way.

When I went into active-duty military, I was relieved to find that the stereotypical leadership style I experienced in my Officer Basic Course wasn't a forced requirement. New lieutenants who led their platoon by yelling were not effective. Platoon leader is typically your first job as a combat arms officer. From day one, the soldiers you're leading have had more experience than you. My platoon sergeant, who reported to me, had been in the Army for fifteen years. And the other noncommissioned officers (NCOs) reporting to him, the section chiefs, had been in for over ten years. Even the youngest private had been in the active Army longer than me. I was fortunate my NCOs were total professionals. If I had shown up yelling and using command authority, especially with my lack of experience, it wouldn't have gone well, and they wouldn't have mentored me to become an effective Army officer.

I saw many of my fellow lieutenants show up using the "motivation" techniques they were trained to use, and the results never ended up working out well. On the surface, it would appear to work. The NCOs and soldiers would obey their orders (with their eyes rolling into the back of their heads when their new officer wasn't looking), even when their commanding officer made poor decisions based on their lack of experience. There was no collaboration, no feedback, and no shared vision of how to achieve the mission. Since we were in a training environment, they were more than happy to watch their leader fail.

One of my fellow lieutenants showed up on his first day and did a surprise inspection of the armory. In the military, taking care of your equipment is something that's taken very seriously. Night vision goggles, when stored, should have their batteries taken out. Every now and then, that wouldn't happen. He knew this. He walked over to the stored night vision goggles, picked a few up until he found one that was a little heavier than the others, opened the battery compartment, and let the forgotten batteries fall to the floor. He then locked up (made to stand at attention) the armory sergeant and gave him the same "motivating talk" my tactical officer gave me. Of course, it ended up with a hearty "Yes, sir!" from the sergeant as the new lieutenant walked away.

Funny thing, karma exists in the military. A year later, the lieutenant's unit was deployed on a training exercise in Thailand. As they were loading up the plane to return, there was the standard inventory of sensitive items such as weapons, communication equipment, and, you guessed it, night vision goggles. Losing a sensitive item is something that draws attention from the entire command. Soldiers are told to stop everything they're doing, and the entire unit searches for the missing item. They searched for three days all around the base and in the jungle where they had trained for a month. As it turned out, this lieutenant accidentally put the night vision goggles in his duffel bag that was loaded first on the plane and forgotten. It was the last place they looked. He was relieved of his position and sent to be the officer in charge of the recreational facility.

While there is undoubtedly a time and place for creating a significant emotional event, those moments are usually reserved for situations that are potentially life-or-death training mistakes or a clear insubordination toward authority. When I was a commander, my unit was on a run, and one of my soldiers in the back began to walk. Clearly, he needed some motivation. I watched with curiosity as my first sergeant approached the soldier. I was sure I was about to witness a significant emotional event, which would have been warranted in this case. Instead, he politely told the soldier and subsequently the rest of the unit to follow him. He walked with the soldier and the rest of the unit behind him wondering what was going to happen next. He sent a soldier to retrieve a stool from our barracks and placed it in the middle of the grass field we found ourselves standing in. He had another soldier go to the dining facility and bring back a large bag of doughnuts.

The soldier had to eat the doughnuts while my first sergeant led the rest of the unit through a grueling workout. They watched him eat those doughnuts while they were smoked in one of the more aggressive workouts I had witnessed at that point in my military career. It took me a few minutes to realize what was going on, but once I saw the look of disdain in the eyes of those soldiers being smoked as they looked at this private on a stool eating doughnuts, I understood. My first sergeant was using influence. The influence of the unit, which I imagine came to life that evening when the lights went out in the barracks. That private never fell behind on a run again.

My first sergeant decided to bypass the traditional significant emotional event. That method had been tried on this private many times and had proven ineffective. Instead, he chose a solution-oriented approach to the problem that used influence. While harsh, the gravity of the situation may not be apparent to someone not in the military. In a combat arms unit, these types of issues, if not addressed effectively, would have spread to others in the unit. That's not acceptable if you're training for a combat situation where actions and attitudes displayed by that private would have certainly cost lives.

Using influence instead of control whenever possible allowed my teams to complete a series of highly successful missions. I became one of the youngest commanders in the Army after four years of leadership training from those who reported to me. I'm forever grateful to both officers who reported to me and, more importantly, my NCOs who taught me that using the necessary influence based on the situation is more effective than using the power of authority.

Situational leadership requires different forms of influence. Sometimes you need to use your position to make tough decisions that you know are right but few agree. I learned a saying from one of my mentors in the Army who created an amazing culture in his unit. His soldiers would run through walls for him (literally). His saying was "Your agreement is optional. Your support is not." He set a tone using influence to make sure that everyone would get behind him when a tough decision needed to be made. He didn't use his power. He created a culture in his unit that everyone understood and agreed that they would follow him, *especially* when they didn't agree. Because of that culture in his unit, there weren't any significant emotional events during challenging moments. Just 100 percent buy-in, even if they disagreed. In those moments, they weren't following him because of his position of authority. They all made a conscious decision in advance as a cohesive team to follow their leader, especially when they didn't want to. That's influence. That's leadership.

HAVE A GROWTH MINDSET

How far can a person with a mindset entrenched in one ideology, one set of social beliefs, one set of "this is how it should be done," with no willingness to step back and see an alternate perspective go in life? Think about people you know who have lived the same life in the same way for the past five or ten years. If all their beliefs, experiences, and the way they live their life are the same, they have a fixed mindset, and if you check in with them ten years from now, they'll still be cycling through life in the same exact way. Intentional disruption cannot occur with a fixed mindset. Intentional disruption requires a growth mindset.

People with growth mindsets thrive on learning, growing, expanding, and moving outside their comfort zone. They welcome new experiences and jump at new opportunities. They enjoy moving toward a goal rather than achieving that goal. Their happiness depends on personal growth, not an outcome.

Stanford psychologist Carol Dweck's research into fixed and growth mindsets is perfectly laid out in her book *Mindset: The New Psychology of Success*. In *Mindset*, she explains that a "fixed mindset" assumes that our character, intelligence, and creative ability are static givens that we are unable to change in any meaningful way. A growth mindset thrives on challenge and sees failure "not as evidence of unintelligence but as a heartening springboard for growth and for stretching our existing abilities." She continues, "I've seen so many people with this one consuming goal of proving themselves—in the classroom, in their careers, and in their relationships. Every situation calls for a confirmation of their intelligence, personality, or character. Every situation is evaluated: Will I succeed or fail? Will I look smart or dumb? Will I be accepted or rejected? Will I feel like a winner or a loser?"

> People with growth mindsets thrive on learning, growing, expanding, and moving outside their comfort zone.

I love her analogy of trying to convince everyone you have a royal flush when you're secretly worried it's a pair of tens. She explains that with a growth mindset, "the hand you're dealt is just the starting point for development. This growth mindset is based on the belief that your basic qualities are things you can cultivate through your efforts." With a growth mindset, you're not afraid to make mistakes, fail spectacularly, and chart new paths for yourself.

A growth mindset offers you the freedom to look at life through your own internal lens rather than seeking external influences and validation. Moving away from those external influences that we are bombarded with on a daily basis, telling us what we should think consciously and subconsciously, is a challenge, but it can be done. When you shed yourself of fixed ideologies and beliefs that don't serve you and understand you have the power to impact your emotions by choosing how you look at yourself and the world around you, a growth mindset that equips you for intentional disruption begins to develop.

Takeaways

- Disruptors are introspective. They understand that to disrupt on a larger scale, they must first disrupt themselves.

- Intentional disruption means creating long-term positive personal change for the sake of creating external positive change.

- Disruptors create purpose.

- Leadership is influence.

- Embrace a growth mindset.

- Intentional disruptors look to the future, appreciate disruption from others, focus on solutions rather than obstacles, create proactive change, and practice self-awareness and self-compassion.

Action Items

- Where can you use disruption in your life?

- What is preventing you from disrupting in these areas?

- Consider how you view the status quo. Then list what you dislike about it and how you might effect its change.

- Think of a problem that you're facing. Then list creative ways of going through it for long-lasting change.

- What is your own vision of the future?

- What about your current mindset needs to change to get there?

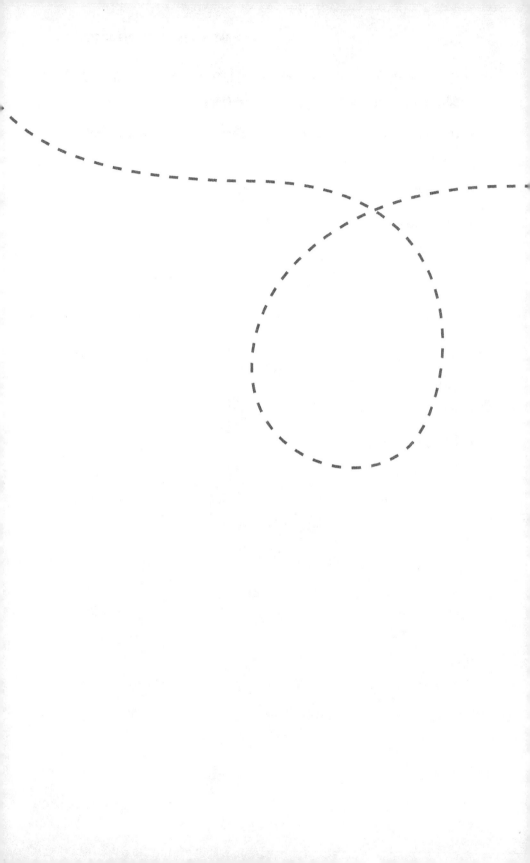

CHAPTER 2

Find Your Different

What is right is not always popular, and what
is popular is not always right.

—ALBERT EINSTEIN

STATEMENTS OF AN INTENTIONAL DISRUPTOR

On a scale of 1–5, with 1 being the least, rate your relatability to the following statements:

_____ I am aware of my beliefs and where they've come from.

_____ I am influenced by others and what they say/think about me.

_____ I can state my *Why* in a sentence and return to it often.

_____ I spend a significant time trying to capitalize on my strengths.

Are you ready to start disrupting yourself?

About five years ago, I found out that my ADD diagnosis a couple of decades before was incorrect. When I moved to Atlanta in 2013, my new doctor prescribed me Adderall to help with my ADD. While I never saw it as a problem, he did. I looked at it as a gift that made me highly creative, and I had learned to be functional with it and harness the positive aspects. Nonetheless, I took his advice and began taking Adderall. At first, it was pretty amazing. I was getting more done in an hour than I would usually get done in four. A massive increase in productivity sure seemed like a positive thing. Until it wasn't.

I later learned amphetamines have that effect on everyone. Amphetamines can take many forms, prescribed as Adderall and Ritalin, among others. It's also found in another form: crystallized methamphetamine hydrochloride or crystal meth. You don't have to be a meth head to abuse amphetamines. Many college students take unprescribed Adderall as a study aid to stay awake and suppress appetites. It's similar in function to cocaine but with a slower onset and longer duration.

While I was on a small dose, over the next few years, I began compensating for the uppers I was on during the day with alcohol at night to sleep. I wasn't aware this was happening, and it took a few years and a meltdown to understand I was essentially doing uppers and downers. While I wasn't aware of the cause of my heavy drinking, I was mindful of the toll it was putting on my body and relationships. I have one son, Paige. We're incredibly close, and he's my motivation for writing this book and sharing my thoughts and stories. He was training for a pentathlon when he was fourteen and asked me to go swimming with him every morning at six o'clock. While I could function with my heavy drinking and get up early in the morning for work, I knew there was no way I could get up at five thirty and go to the pool and swim for an hour and a half.

Up until that point, he and I had done everything together. As he became a teenager, a friend gave me some of the best advice I've received. They told me that if I wanted to maintain a close relationship with Paige, I needed to meet him where he was at. They further explained that he was happy to follow Daddy around as a small boy and do whatever I was doing, but that wasn't going to last now that he was a teenager. I quit drinking that day.

I began getting up at 5:30 a.m. and swimming with Paige. We still look back on our time together, grabbing Starbucks on the way to the pool, competitively racing almost every lap (we're competitive about everything with each other), and grabbing breakfast at a nearby café afterward.

While one problem was solved, another one emerged. As my body began to heal from several years of heavy drinking, I was still on Adderall, and I began to sleep less and less. Six months later, I went without sleep for four days. After my first night of not being able to sleep, I went on a five-mile run at 6:00 a.m. and felt fantastic. Three days later, I had only taken a two-hour unfulfilling nap. I began hallucinating from sleep deprivation. I'd experienced this when I was in the Army and in the field for several weeks with very little sleep or food. But this was different. I was in my comfortable house looking at a backpack in my office that I swore had some small animal in it moving around. I looked at the trash can in my office and saw green smoke coming out of it. I even took a video of it and watched it afterward, only to see a regular trash can and no green smoke.

I reported my condition to my doctor who had prescribed the Adderall, and he promptly referred me to a psychiatrist, who didn't take long to determine that I was bipolar, not ADD. My specific diagnosis is bipolar II. Many of the symptoms of ADD and bipolar II are similar. While bipolar I usually lands you in the hospital and results in highly erratic behavior, bipolar II is less severe. My emotional thermostat is broken as a result of my bipolar disorder. When most people experience emotions such as fear, anxiety, elation, and joy, their brain can keep those emotions in check, like the thermostat in your house. When things get too hot, the AC turns on. When things start to get too cold, the heat kicks in to return the house temperature to normal. My thermostat lets my hot and cold get to uncomfortable levels before it kicks in.

It turns out there are two things that are *really* bad for anyone suffering from bipolar disorder—amphetamines and alcohol. I had solved for the latter, but that action had put my thermostat in a continual state of "hot." Removing Adderall from the equation was the next step, along with medication for bipolar II (which is interestingly the same medication used for people who have seizures). Finally, I started to feel "normal." However, after some introspection on all those events, I realized I was far from normal. My brain didn't work like others. It was unordinary.

A funny thing happened. I was relieved. I always knew I was different, and now I fully understood why. There is a bonus to having a mental illness. Your other medication includes exercise, great sleep, and eating clean. As I focused on those "medications," a clear picture of who I was began to emerge. All the experiences of my life and how I approached them began to make sense. I fully understood why I was different from others. It was a fantastic feeling to be able to approach my severe feelings of fear, anxiety, and doubt with a clear perspective.

You don't have to get diagnosed with a mental illness to fully realize who you are and why you're different. I took the long path on that one.

You're Not Normal

I am the oldest of five kids, and my mother always introduced me as the weird one. My boundless drive and focus were not considered normal teenage attributes—it's not considered normal for most adults either—I am perfectly OK with that.

Jack Daly, entrepreneur, leading sales speaker and trainer, and author, is a man who knows how to embrace his different. At just thirteen, Jack envisioned where he wanted to be by the age of thirty in all aspects of his life, including educational, financial, professional, and familial. With his unique internal drive, he interviewed two hundred successful businesspeople to learn how they acquired their success and what advice they could lend to a thirteen-year-old boy wanting to map out his life.

Fast-forward to forty-six and Jack found it was time to push the boundaries of normal even further. The kids were grown; he sold his businesses and took a year off. He opened himself up to a new opportunity in business and ran his first marathon in that time. Jack chose to purposefully disrupt his life to begin a career in public speaking and coaching CEOs while pushing the limits of his physical abilities through marathons and Ironmans. Today Jack has run marathons in all fifty states and has completed more than fifteen full Ironmans. Oh, and at age fifty-eight, he had to learn how to swim before he could do the Ironman.

I believe in solutions over obstacles. All I see when I look in the mirror is a face and a guy. I guess I just don't see the obstacles; they're there, but I'm about accomplishing and checking the box, so if I make the wrong turn, I just have to find my way back on course. At fifty-eight, I didn't know how to swim, but I had competing in an Ironman on my bucket list for two decades, and a 2.4-mile swim is how it starts. Now I have completed fifteen Ironmans, including a world championship in Hawaii. In Hawaii, the bike riding is three loops, and after the first loop, I was leading comfortably in my age group. (I need that to win.) But the next two laps, I had three flat tires, and I only carry two tubes. Three flats and two tubes doesn't work, so I think about quitting, but I don't have the quit gene. It was two miles to an aid station, and I walked there carrying the bike, changed the tire, and was back in the race at the back of the pack. Clearly, I'm not going to win my age group.

One hundred and twenty miles in and now I have a 26.2-mile run. Emotionally you want to put the bike in the rack and call it a day, but I'm there to cross the finish line. I started with the mindset that I would cross the finish line. So I leave the bike behind, and I run those miles, and I chalk it up to life. Setbacks happen all the time. Business speakers will tell you how successful they are, but all of them have an ugly story about how life throws curveballs at them. You can quit or pull up your pants and get after it; it's plain and simple for me.

Today Jack sits down with his own personal board of coaches and makes a detailed blueprint for his life each year.

When I turned sixty, I decided to put together a photo book called "A Year in the Life of Jack Daly"—a daily photograph of something going on in my life. It changes your game when every morning you find yourself wondering, "What am I going to do today that will make a memorable photo?" I didn't want to accumulate hundreds of photos of me sitting at a desk!

We love the word normal. It's used so often that it seems, well, normal. In 2018, "The Myth of Optimality in Clinical Neuroscience" paper was published in *Trends in Cognitive Sciences* journal.[1] The authors, Yale University neuroscientists Avram Holmes and Lauren Patrick, explain why we must move beyond the traditional concept of "normal." They argue that normal doesn't exist and explain our brains don't do uniformity. Each of us thinks, feels, and processes differently. Hence, there is no normal. Yet humans need to put things that are different into rule-based buckets. Normal is just the average behavior across a large population. Anything outside the average is put into a bucket with a name. A name with negative connotations.

Since Holmes and Patrick released the valve on the normal pressure cooker, let's talk about what it means to be different. Being different means you're not ordinary, so the pursuit of being *extraordinary* is fruitless. Instead, if you have the courage, you possess the ability to be your authentic self—to be unordinary. A self that is radically different from what is believed to be normal in any group setting you find yourself. *Incredibly* different from those who are doing their best every day to be normal. It means that you embrace your true self and live your life the way *you* want to live it.

Let's look at mental illness. It's not normal, right? It's a broken mind. As I said earlier, my emotional thermostat doesn't function like others. But I'm not alone. According to the World Health Organization, mental disorders affect one in four people.[2] That's a lot of disorders. So what percentage needs to be reached for it not to be a disorder? Clearly, it's higher than 25 percent.

The National Institute of Mental Health estimates 4.4 percent of adults experience bipolar disorder at some time in their life.[3] While any brain illness can cause serious problems, it's not all bad news. Psychologists have associated dyslexia with more original thinking, autism with pattern identification, and bipolar disorder, with its mania and depression, with perseverance. With all their significant challenges, these mental diagnostic buckets can be superpowers. In the paper "Mental Disorders in the Entrepreneurship Context: When Being Different Can Be an Advantage," the authors cite research that shows a strong connection between psychological disorders and entrepreneurship, finding positive associations between entrepreneurship and dyslexia, bipolar, and other mood disorders.[4]

Many of the great leaders and artists we have come to admire would have been diagnosed in today's society with mental illness. Abraham Lincoln suffered from clinical depression. Nikola Tesla was severely obsessive-compulsive. Vincent van Gogh was bipolar, epileptic, and schizophrenic. Wolfgang Mozart had Tourette's syndrome. Michelangelo had both obsessive-compulsive disorder and high-functioning autism. Charles Dickens suffered from severe depression. Isaac Newton, Teddy Roosevelt, and Beethoven are now believed to have been bipolar. Winston Churchill (who was also bipolar), Aristotle, and even Moses (based on scripture references in Exodus) suffered from stuttering. None of these people used their disorders as an excuse. Instead, they used their natural state of being unordinary to create powerful change in the world.

It's believed Aristotle once said, "No great genius has existed without a strain of madness." My favorite definition of normal is from Pulitzer Prize–winning author Ellen Goodman. She said, "Normal is getting dressed in clothes that you buy for work and driving through traffic in a car that you are still paying for—to get to the job you need to pay for the clothes and the car, and the house you leave vacant all day so you can afford to live in it." When you look at *Merriam-Webster's* several definitions of normal, you must really question why you'd ever want to be normal. The first definition is "conforming to a type, standard, or regular pattern" and then followed by "characterized by average intelligence or development" and my personal favorite, "free from mental illness: mentally sound."

Why would you want to conform to a regular pattern and be characterized by average intelligence or development? Think about all that would be lost if Lincoln, Dickens, Michelangelo, and others had not embraced their different. In a world that insists on learning through conformity and existing universal knowledge, Einstein dared to say "Imagination is more important than knowledge. For knowledge is limited to all we now know and understand, while imagination embraces the entire world, and all there ever will be to know and understand." Find your different by re-tapping into the imagination and curiosity you had as a child. You'll quickly find you're not normal, and you're in good company.

> Why would you want to conform to a regular pattern and be characterized by average intelligence or development?

Rule Breakers

Humans are very good at creating rules to make sense of the world. Without rules, it would be hard to understand the world and ourselves. When we're kids, we form rules to separate things such as colors, sounds, and even that bully on the playground from the kid you want to invite over on a playdate. However, the development of those rules can have a detrimental effect on a person's ability to express themselves and understand who they really are. Our differences often break the rules we've accepted within the culture we've been raised in. Bad and good become clearly defined by rules. Sometimes rules that define bad are wrong. The trick is to identify those rules and break them.

In our adolescence, we try to push away from these rules. This doesn't usually go well. We quickly learn to follow the rules of what's considered normal, or we're punished, labeled as weird, or worse. The identity we form is solidified as we develop into "fully formed adults." Creativity and imagination are taken from us as we instead create what we're taught is a stable personality. I think most adults fear using their imagination because they're afraid of where it may take them. But if you reflect on that fear, think about this: imagination is just dreaming, and no one ever dies in their dreams. There isn't really anything to be afraid of when you imagine.

What if you chose to go back and examine with curiosity who you were naturally growing up? I'll bet you'll find a bunch of pieces of yourself you left along the way. When you look at the lives of Harriet Tubman, Jane Austen, Rosa Parks, and Susan B. Anthony, you'll notice at some point they stopped following the rules, and they changed the course of history. Some of the most famous and influential rule breakers are women and minorities. They have a tremendous number of rules put on them from the day they are born.

To properly break the rules, you need to be authentic, which works out nicely because you can't be authentic if you follow other people's rules. You can't be authentic if you're trying to be like everyone else. However, authenticity doesn't get you all the way to understanding your different. It just gives you the freedom to find it.

Q&A WITH DISRUPTOR KAT COLE

Kat Cole has broken all the rules, and she's done it with authenticity. At seventeen, Kat began working as a hostess at Hooters. Knowing that wasn't the only thing she wanted to do, she jumped into all aspects of the business—bartending, cooking, and eventually training and hiring staff. It wasn't long before management recognized her hard work and natural business acumen and asked her to help open their first location in

Australia. The nineteen-year-old, having never ventured out of the state of Florida, said "Hell yes!" and in three days secured her passport and was on a plane to Australia. Kat's "Hell yes!" began her glass-shattering, rule-breaking journey to becoming one of today's top thought leaders not only in business but also in her compassionate view of what really matters in the world.

Q: What has been the most significant disruption you have made in how business gets done?

A: One of the most significant changes we made as a team at Cinnabon was embracing this idea of multichannel and having products that were sold, not just in our legacy business but in grocery stores and restaurants, and from there building an omnichannel branded product ecosystem. It was a vastly different way of building a brand and a method that was unfamiliar to our team and the marketplace. Still, it turned out to be wildly successful and continues to be a way of doing business that is unique and remains strong in our company and across our brands today.

Q: What were the primary hurdles that you came across, and how did you overcome those?

A: One was understanding that these were new channels and new products showing up in new places and recognizing that people were unfamiliar and fearful of what that might mean for the brand and unsure of whether or not it would positively or negatively impact their business. I overcame that by finding the coalition of the willing. The people who were willing to test and learn with me with a mindset of adding value to the whole business and not just creating value in one area of the business. Through the process, we really celebrated the wins. We made sure that when the new business grew, we took some of the proceeds from that business and reinvested it into the core business as a thank-you for their support and engagement and as an acknowledgment that all areas of the business are connected. We put our money where our mouth is to support the legacy business.

Q: How do you calculate your risks when embarking on a new path?

A: I evaluate numbers, volumes, customers, and channels. I review consumer research and gain an understanding of what people buy when and where, and I think deeply about how that will all come together. It's about research and connecting with consumers and other stakeholders like our franchisees and establishing a good point of view on how things will come together and what they might look like when they all shape up in the marketplace. Those combined components will tell us if there is actual risk and what the perceived risks are. We need to address the emotion and concern of those risks and put safeguards into place as appropriate.

Q: You've spoken on conscious capitalism. Can you talk a bit about how that is disrupting the way we do business?

A: There have been a variety of thought leaders coming from businesses for decades talking about the fact that there are critical stakeholders other than just the shareholder. This idea is definitely not new, but there are evolutions of those ideas that suggest different ways that for-profit businesses can and should go to market by taking better care of multiple stakeholders and not solely focused on highest returns to shareholders at all costs, because that's proving to be unsustainable. The most sustainable way to provide returns to shareholders and sustain value creation in a brand is, in fact, to take the best care of key stakeholders: employees, the community, customers, and people working in the value chain, like vendors.

Q: What's an example of how you practice that at Focus Brands?

A: For Focus Brands, it's how we think about investing in our community. It might be our diversity and inclusion and equity initiatives across the company to ensure the employees we have represent the customers we have and want to have. It's ensuring that we have the highest quality vendor partners and that they're conducting business in a high-integrity way, not just the lowest cost of things we can get.

Our Java brand is an example of this thought process. We saw that it was essential to move to more plant-based protein and a variety of healthier snacks. It isn't the cheapest thing for us to do. It's quite expensive to bring in more premium proteins and plant-based proteins with a focus on more natural and organic options. We had to have the conversation that yes, it's going to cost more, but it's the right thing to do in order to allow the companies making those products and ingredients grow and to delight our customers on their own journey to be healthier and that ultimately, we will build a better brand as a result. We chose quality over pure profit.

Q: Through your humanitarian work, you have developed a real presence in the nonprofit world. Do you see yourself as a disruptor in that arena as well? And if so, how?

A: The global, humanitarian mindset that I bring to my for-profit work is a natural fit for nonprofits. Combining that view with my entrepreneurial expertise, I can help nonprofits be a bit scrappier. It's about providing them the knowledge and tools to leverage technology that enables them to do their work in a new way and add value to their communities. In addition, I bring a business mindset to the nonprofit world, which historically isn't known for having an entrepreneurial spirit.

Q: You clearly have a lot on your plate. How do you orient yourself and take stock?

A: I reflect regularly. I've challenged myself to think about what someone else would do in my role, to look at my world with a fresh perspective, and to align that with my values and use that to motivate me to continually evolve into the woman I am becoming.

Aside from not following the rules, authentic people don't have a fixed ideology. Ideology, by definition, is a set of social rules and beliefs shared by a collective group. To be clear, faith in God is not an ideology. *Merriam-Webster* defines faith as "complete trust or confidence in someone or something." It defines ideology as "the integrated assertions, theories, and aims that constitute a sociopolitical program." See the difference and how we confuse them? One is trust based, and the other is rule based.

The more rules, the less chance you have of being authentic when following that ideology. And most ideologies have a large number of rules and beliefs. And over time, even more are added. So much so they usually split off into smaller groups who have a slightly different version of the original ideology. Those splits and the splits that follow create anger and resentment toward each other who haven't embraced their chosen new version. In mild cases, they lead to unproductive social media screaming matches. I don't need to give you examples. You already get it. You're probably living it.

What if you didn't have to fit into any ideology? What if you could believe some of one but not all of it? What if you could change your mind about those beliefs as you receive new information from others and life experiences? It's more challenging than you think. Fixed mindsets are very compelling since we naturally want to fit in by following the rules. Growth mindsets open the door for creativity unbound by rules. They also lead to less anger and resentment and more happiness.

Find Yourself and Your Why

Finding yourself means connecting to your essential nature *and* nurture. Who are you? What do you like? What do you dislike? How does your personal history shape you? This last point is critical. As we grow up, we're influenced by numerous people and various social norms. These influences contribute to the beliefs we develop about ourselves and our surroundings. Because our thoughts influence our feelings and our feelings influence our actions and our actions influence our results, we need to constantly interrogate them. I was greatly influenced by my parents and upbringing, but as an adopted child, I also wanted to find my biological self and nature.

I first began a search for my birth mother when I was a junior in college. It took the adoption agency a few years to find her because the records were sealed, and back then the simple genealogy online searches weren't available. During that time, I had joined the Army, something I had wanted to do from a very young age. When it came time to choose my branch, my first choice was artillery. Who wouldn't want to blow stuff up with big bullets? In addition, unlike other branches, artillery officers have the opportunity to do a variety of jobs in their career: platoon leader, fire direction officer, and forward observer, to name a few. After college, I was commissioned as a second lieutenant and reported for my officer advanced course in Fort Sill, Oklahoma. The mecca for artillery. All army artillery soldiers and Marines spend their training time in Fort Sill. Officers and enlisted from other countries also come to Fort Sill to learn artillery.

A couple of years later, when I was stationed in Hawaii, I was notified of my birth mother's name and contact information, and I wrote her a letter. (Email wasn't widely used in 1995, and long-distance calls were expensive.) She wrote back, and we arranged to meet when I was home for the holidays. It turned out she lived in Virginia Beach, not far from my parents' house in Fredericksburg, Virginia. I put on a coat and tie, borrowed my dad's car, and nervously arrived at my birth mother's house with flowers in hand.

We were sitting across from each other at dinner, and she quietly asked me, "Well, what do you do?" I told her I was in the Army. "What do you do in the Army?" she asked. When I told her I was an artillery officer, her face went white. She stared at me for a long, awkward moment. Then she said, "You come from a long line of West Point Field Artillery Officers." She went on to tell me that my great-great-grandfather was Gen. William Josiah Snow. I knew all about General Snow. He was a legend in artillery. He modernized artillery during World War I to become the first chief of the Field Artillery. I passed by his portrait in Snow Hall every day during my six months at Fort Sill. I remembered that portrait because, on numerous occasions, my buddies used to joke that he looked like me with a mustache. I also learned that my family had a long history of mental illness. It was a passing thought at the time, as I wasn't yet aware of my own diagnosis, and I assumed it related to other members of my family tree—not the successful line of generals and military officers. That turned out not to be the case.

We are a combination of our nature and our nurture. My mom and dad raised me in a loving, nurturing environment. They taught me so much and significantly influenced the foundation of my beliefs and the person I have become. Then there is my biological nature that has also influenced who I am and the way I think. For most people, nature and nurture are one package. I received the gift of both individually.

When you venture out into the world, you are exposed to a multitude of thoughts and beliefs that differ from yours. I think it's essential to be open to them as you continually examine your own. I like the analogy of storing your beliefs in a backpack. On a regular basis, unpack that backpack, look at each belief, and really question it. Look at what you believe and *why* you believe it's both true and essential. It doesn't mean you're constantly discarding your beliefs. It simply means you're stress testing them to make sure you still honestly believe them.

Growing up, I remember the way people looked at me when I shared my ideas. They looked at me as if I was the odd one, making me feel like I was from another world. That no longer concerns me. I am from another world. Today I see myself as someone who creates new worlds, ideas, thoughts, and actions different from the status quo. Most of them have led to spectacular failures and learnings.

Challenging your thoughts and beliefs and going through true self-discovery is terrifying, but you can build a tolerance for the process. I know because I do it whenever possible. It's scary to ignore the voice that says you're not smart enough, good-looking enough, or capable enough to be yourself. It's hard to ignore the voice that says you should take that safe job, you should stick with who and what you know, do what makes you feel comfortable and instead tune into the voice that says what you really need. These expectations and narratives

> Challenging your thoughts and beliefs and going through true self-discovery is terrifying, but you can build a tolerance for the process.

instill a fear within us that creates a giant psychological obstacle to becoming ourselves. But you can move through that obstacle if you commit to giving self-discovery a concentrated, courageous effort. What you'll find on the other side is nothing short of spectacular.

We all have goals of what we want, but not everyone has a vision of where they want to be. Your vision is critical to developing meaningful goals. We have all been asked the question, where do you see yourself in one year, five years, and ten years? And then we make a list. But instead of writing a list, we need to draw it out to reveal what's truly important to us in the most simplistic way possible.

VISION EXERCISE

A few years ago, I did an exercise with a group of seven franchise CEO founders I started with Nick Freidman, cofounder of College Hunks Hauling Junk. We met for four hours every month to push ourselves by exploring the top and bottom 5 percent of our lives personally, professionally, and in our relationships with our families and friends. We did this through experience sharing and sometimes extremely thought-provoking exercises. This is one that was particularly impactful for me.

Grab some crayons and four sheets of colored construction paper. Spend five minutes on each sheet, drawing a picture of what you want your life to be like in five years, ten years, fifteen years, and twenty years from now. Drawing it out using crayons and construction paper forces you to do a big picture overview and doesn't allow you to dive into the small details that don't matter. You draw stick figures and a beach and sunshine and family instead of getting caught up in making it a beautiful picture. It's a representation of what you see yourself doing. Draw the big things that truly matter. Draw your *Why*.

My childlike drawings were pictures telling stories of my family and other meaningful relationships. I didn't include a cool car, a bigger house, or any material things. I didn't have anything other than relationships and experiences with those I love and care about. Deep down, we know what matters. Stuff can be taken away, but your experiences can't; it's those experiences that build impactful relationships. Sometimes it takes some construction paper and crayons to figure that out. I still have those pictures. I look at them from time to time when I'm particularly stressed about something that's superficial (most things are).

While you're seeking your true self, remember to avoid attaching your identity to outcomes. What happens if I identify myself as an outstanding salesperson, and I miss my 2020 targets? My motivation to achieve my 2021 targets declines. Why? Because there's no true purpose behind achieving that goal. Purpose should always govern outcomes. It should always define your *Why*.

There are times when we reach what we thought were our *Whys*, only to find we have veered far off course, and we need to reassess who and where we truly want to be. For David Panton, it was a devastating and undeniable realization. David is a graduate of Princeton and Harvard Law School. He was the second Black president of the Harvard Law Review. The first was Barack Obama.

I was on top of the world. Here I was in my late twenties, married to a beautiful woman, father to a beautiful son, head of the largest private equity firm in the Caribbean, head of the largest young professional organization in Jamaica, and appointed to the Jamaica Senate, when my world crashed down upon me. My wife decided she didn't want to be married to me anymore, and a grueling divorce ensued. I had a falling-out with my business partner and sold my share of the business to him. As everything began to fall around me, I made the decision to resign from the Senate. In twelve months, I went from the top of the world with a bright and well laid out future in front of me to having no idea what I would be doing in the next week or month.

I knew that I really had to look inside myself to figure out a way forward. I needed to disrupt myself and my life. I did that by retreating to two essential foundations in my life that I had neglected during my successful ascent to everything I thought I wanted. My faith and my family. I went back to church. I started reading my Bible again and becoming more in tune with my faith. I also moved back in with my parents. Not because I needed a physical home but because I needed that connection and support. My father fell ill during that time and subsequently died of cancer. I was glad to have had that time with him.

I also spent more time with my sister and brother. Two years later, while visiting my sister and brother-in-law in Atlanta, I decided to make a fresh start there. It was an anxious time for me. I'd been an entrepreneur for the previous five years, and now I was having to look for a job—to work for someone else in a location that I was unfamiliar with and had no connections in. I did my due diligence and researched the private equity firms in Atlanta, and I cold-called the senior partner of the largest firm, Larry Mott of Merlin Ventures. I was apprehensive, but I was also confident in my background.

David got the job. Seven months later, the parent company of Merlin Ventures decided they were going to shut down. David was the last person in, and therefore he knew he would be the first one out if he didn't act.

I approached Larry and said, "Larry, this is an opportunity for you to be entrepreneurial. I've been entrepreneurial with a private equity firm, so I can be helpful," and he agreed. And he chose four people to partner with him, and I was one of the four. And the rest of it, as they say, is history.

Years later, David remains focused on his *Why*.

I practice humility. I believe I am wiser, and I am far more accepting of what happens to me. Having been through what I've been through and the high cost of that ambition, and coming out the other side, I know that no matter what, there's another side. I credit self-reflection and self-disruption with the strong relationships I now have with my sons, my former wife, my mother, and my siblings. I continue to nurture my faith, and I am very active in my church. These are the foundations that keep me grounded in my true Why and purpose.

One of my favorite Simon Sinek quotes from his book *Find Your Why* is "There are two ways to build a career or a business. We can go through life hunting and pecking, looking for opportunities or customers, hoping that something connects. Or we can go through life with intention, knowing what our piece looks like, knowing our why, and going straight to the places we fit." We often search for how to do things, but to achieve lasting change and reach long-term goals, we have to understand *why* we're doing what we're doing. We have to understand our purpose.

I don't start companies to generate wealth. That's a goal, not my *Why*. I start companies because I like solving challenging problems, and I love building something through developing relationships with people. In business, my *Why* is simple: create something that will have a lasting impact on our customers and those who build the company. In my personal life, my *Why* is to continue disrupting myself to keep upgrading my potential to connect with those I lead and love.

If you don't know who you are or why you're doing what you're doing, how can you make any decisions? How can you decide when to say no? How can you determine if you've reached a goal? How can you even set a goal that matters? You can't. Instead of pointing yourself in a direction, you'll find yourself spinning in a circle, searching for meaning.

Ultimately, man should not ask what the meaning of his life is, but rather must recognize that it is he who is asked. In a word, each man is questioned by life; and he can only answer to life by answering for his own life; to life he can only respond by being responsible.
—VIKTOR E. FRANKL, *MAN'S SEARCH FOR MEANING*

Without purpose, we can't reach our outcomes. Without purpose, we are literally meaningless. When you know who you are and you've identified the values that establish your *Why*, you will live a happy life. As Frankl put it, "Those who have a 'why' to live, can bear with almost any 'how.'"

Finding yourself helps you find your purpose, enabling you to find your passion, which allows you to find meaningful opportunities.

Access Your Ignorance

One way to find who you are is to explore who you're not. One of the most effective ways of doing this is by assessing your strengths and weaknesses. This takes a lot of courage. After all, who wants to focus on the things they're *not* good at? We don't like to look at our weaknesses because they generate a large amount of uncertainty and doubt. This leads to fear, and fear makes people uncomfortable. I suggest that you go to that uncomfortable place by identifying your weaknesses and then really sitting with them. It's OK to have weaknesses. Everyone does. We do some of our best learning from a place of weakness.

Keith Schroeder, founder of High Road Craft Brands, was forced to identify what others might see as his weaknesses through his work as a chef. "There's an intensity to working in close physical proximity to people. If you don't have chemistry, you lose your temper, and you feel like crowding each other out. In this situation, I understood what about me was appealing to others, and what about me was repulsive to others. Then you try to correct certain behaviors so you can create flow with those people. When you achieve flow, there's a platonic kind of romance that takes place in the dance of making something together while in close quarters."

So many authors and business professionals write about attempting to work on weaknesses until they become neutral, if not strong, traits. I disagree with this approach to weakness. Unless you want to be a jack-of-all-trades and master of none, you will have to learn to live with your weaknesses and even embrace them. Trying to "fix" your weaknesses is just another way of avoiding failure. I've noticed that when I put my fears and weaknesses out there instead of hiding them, something incredible happens. I feel free to fail in front of others. Accepting fear as one of my weaknesses rather than trying to improve it gives me permission to fail, which ultimately gives me permission to grow. Rather than focusing on changing them, accept them and focus on your strengths. Your strengths are what drive you toward your goal. Accept your weaknesses, do the best with them that you can, and move forward using your strengths.

Surround Yourself with Inspiring Peers

*Above all, keep a close watch on this—that you are never so tied to
your former acquaintances and friends that you are pulled down to
their level. If you don't, you'll be ruined ... You must choose whether to
be loved by these friends and remain the same person or to become a
better person at the cost of those friends ... if you try to have it both
ways you will neither make progress nor keep what you once had.*
—EPICTETUS, *DISCOURSES*

Jim Rohn famously said that we are the average of the five people we
spend the most time with. I've found that to be true, and as I've continually disrupted myself over the years, I find that I'm not spending
time with the same people.

The people I hang with now all have a growth mindset and a commitment to lifelong learning. I used to outgrow my friends, especially
those in my professional circles, every few years. It was never a hard
stop of friendship, more of a drifting away. They weren't growing, so
we no longer shared the same things in common. Then about six years
ago, I was fortunate enough to join the Young Presidents' Organization
(YPO). It's a group of over thirty thousand CEOs from 142 countries
with $9 trillion in combined revenue employing over twenty-two
million people. To qualify, you have to reach a certain revenue threshold
and number of employees before you're forty-five years old to join. The
entire organization is built around the principle of a commitment to
lifelong learning. We all share a growth mindset. It doesn't matter if
you have a $20 million company or a $1 billion company. We come
together to learn from one another on a level playing field. You never
outgrow friends who are committed to lifelong learning. In fact, all the
stories from others in this book are friends I met in YPO.

Most of us are protective of our physical bodies, yet we casually allow our minds to be influenced by the lowest bidder. Intentional disruptors, on the other hand, are very protective of who they let influence them. They know who they are, they understand why they're moving toward specific goals, and they surround themselves with like-minded people or inspiring peers. And they don't watch cable news.

Inspiring peers challenge you and encourage you to see the world in a different light. As a result, you end up setting the bar for your own outcomes much higher than you would have without the influence of those peers. So how do you find your inspiring peers? You can start by weeding out noninspiring peers. When someone constantly fixates on things out of their control, that's a big red flag you shouldn't be spending time with them. If their default when something goes wrong is to complain or blame, politely walk away. Few people think they have a fixed mindset, but when you start looking for it, you'll find that most do.

> Inspiring peers challenge you and encourage you to see the world in a different light.

As we seek out inspiring peers, we will continue to have noninspiring people in our lives. On the other hand, there will be family and friends who practice a fixed mindset who remain essential to us. Keith Schroeder talks about how he balances the two.

After more than a decade as a chef in high-end restaurants, Keith decided to open an ice cream company to help make the lives of fellow chefs easier. Why? Because he had a poor customer service experience with one of the top ice cream manufacturers when he requested their product for an event he was hosting. He decided that he was probably not the only one receiving this poor service, and he needed to solve the problem. When he shared the exciting news with the people in his life, he received mixed reviews.

There was a tremendous amount of skepticism and worry about his well-being and his state of mind on his family's side. The common questions were, what does this world need with another ice cream company? What makes your idea different? On the flip side, Keith's inner circle of people in the industry were favorable. Their response was that Keith starting a company would be fun and high tech—they were nothing but encouraging. "I learned to compartmentalize the feedback from those two worlds. I think of my own intentions and what I'd like to do, and if I'm disappointed and heartbroken, I accept that as part of the ride." In case you're curious, you can find Keith's ice cream in the freezer section of most grocery stores and famous restaurants.

Whether in business or your personal life, if you want to disrupt and be the best you can be, you have to surround yourself with people who mirror your values, not your beliefs. You have to protect your mind and how it's influenced. Every day you protect your body by looking both ways before crossing the street, eating well, and exercising. Carefully choosing who you spend time with—finding your inspiring peers—puts those same protections in place for your mind.

When you surround yourself with aspiring peers, the fear that we sometimes associate with being our authentic self dissipates. It's much easier to be yourself when the people around you share your values and support your *Why*.

Think like a Child

*Every child is an artist. The problem is how to
remain an artist once we grow up.*
−PABLO PICASSO

When I was a kid, I was insanely curious and creative. When I was four years old, my mom bought me a sewing machine. In 1974, there weren't any "boy" sewing machines. It was a pink Holly Hobbie sewing machine, to be precise. I wasn't old enough to care. She first taught me to sew a cloth carrying bag. It was simple. Take two squares of material, sew the edges in a U-shape, and flip it inside out. A couple of cloth handles and you're done. I was proud of my creation and dashed out the door to show my friends. They were not impressed. I was quickly made fun of for carrying a girl's pocketbook.

I was both devastated and embarrassed. Then I was angry. I quickly picked up a large scoop of gravel from my driveway and put it in said pocketbook. Now it wasn't a pocketbook. As I began to swing it over my head, all the kids ran for the hills behind our house. Thankfully, I wasn't deterred from that experience (and later thankful I never used the weapon I had created on anyone). I continued to create things (this time in private). Needlepoint, cross-stitch, latch hook, crochet, and knitting were my creative outlets. My friends never saw my creations after the first incident. Instead, my mom would give them as gifts to her friends in the church, forever proud of her creative child.

I had successfully learned to hide that different side of me from my peers. When I was in high school, it got worse. I became painfully self-aware of what was considered normal and felt myself focusing more on fitting in instead of pursuing my different. Most high school kids can relate to this feeling. Unfortunately, these insecurities often only grow as we move into adulthood.

The social priming we receive as we move into adulthood creates a disconnect between failure-proof children and failure-avoidant adults. Children are allowed the freedom to be themselves. In fact, they're often encouraged by their parents to *be* distinct. When we're very young, being different doesn't have negative connotations. It doesn't separate us from our tribe. However, when we start going to school, and we're encouraged to streamline our different, that changes. Being really good at one thing, being distinctive, takes a lot of energy. Choosing to spend your energy trying to be normal at everything is encouraged. Encouraging children to be normal is as easy as it is counterproductive.

Today our house is filled with gear from activities that my son has tried and either moved on from or kept trying. We have a piano keyboard, guitar, tennis racket, golf clubs, fencing gear, and the list goes on. Some interests stuck and he's still passionate about them today, but most didn't. We encouraged this massive experimenting phase of his life. We encouraged him to be curious and try new things. Recently, he tried video editing because he helps with the school announcements, which are all digital now. The thing is, he absolutely loves film and editing. Maybe that will stick, but likely, he'll continue to find more passions and interests and leave others behind. We want him to follow his passions and understand that it's perfectly fine if he decides not to go down that road.

What would happen if you approached every day like a child? What if you weren't afraid to fail? Think about how you feel when someone rejects you. Maybe your colleagues shoot down your idea or a peer thinks an idea (especially a good one) is ridiculous. As insignificant as each of these instances of rejection can be, for someone with a fixed mindset, they're devastating. On the other hand, when approached with childlike wonder or a growth mindset, these situations can be incredibly valuable learning experiences. Your mindset defines you.

Another great thing about kids is that they never stop asking questions. They're insanely curious. They don't just play with an electronic toy. They turn it over, they ask why the siren sounds when a certain button is pushed, and they drop it from the top of the stairs to see what happens. Children are elaborative interrogators. They constantly follow any idea with why and how questions. As elaborative interrogators, they think about the relationship between different ideas. They want to understand how ideas are both similar and different from one another. That's why road trips when my son was young never had a quiet moment. As an only child without the distraction of a sibling, he constantly looked out the window, asking, "What's that?" While I sometimes became tired of answering his questions on those long trips, he never tired of asking them. Thankfully.

Consistently using your childlike curiosity to ask questions will help you become insanely different. Curiosity is a muscle. The more you exercise it, the bigger it gets. Geniuses such as Einstein think differently than the average person. He avoided ideology and disliked authority. Most of Einstein's intelligence came from his curiosity, not his IQ. He had a vivid imagination and could do thought experiments in his head to visualize his theories. In fact, he valued imagination over everything else. His imagination allowed him to challenge conventional wisdom (aka knowledge). As he put it, "Imagination is more important than knowledge. For knowledge is limited, whereas imagination embraces the entire world, stimulating progress, giving birth to evolution." Like Einstein, have a healthy suspicion of authority and use your imagination to challenge everything.

Takeaways

- Normal doesn't exist, and our brains don't do uniformity.

- When you choose to be unordinary, you are free to embrace your true self and live your life the way *you* want to live it.

- Your thoughts influence your feelings, your feelings influence your actions, and your actions influence your results.

- Challenging your beliefs and going through the process of true self-discovery is terrifying, but you can build up a tolerance for the process.

- Accept your weaknesses, do the best with them that you can, and move forward using your strengths.

- Inspiring peers challenge you and encourage you to see the world in a different light.

- The social priming we receive as we move into adulthood creates a disconnect between failure-proof children and failure-avoidant adults.

Action Items

- Think back to your childhood and examine with curiosity your natural self growing up. What pieces of yourself did you leave behind? Which ones do you want to get back?

- List three "life rules" you have broken in the past one to five years.

- Identify a long-held belief or ideology you are committed to. Break it down and objectively look at all its components. Now assess honestly what components your authentic self truly ascribes to.

- Identify your weaknesses and then really sit in the discomfort of them.

- List the five people you spend most of your time with. Do they have a growth mindset? Are they inspiring you to grow?

- List three things you could do if you weren't afraid to fail ... and do them.

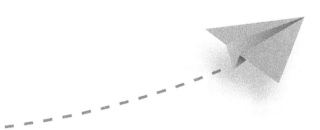

CHAPTER 3

Embrace Your Fears

Many are harmed by fear itself, and many may have
come to their fate while dreading fate.

—SENECA, *OEDIPUS*

STATEMENTS OF AN INTENTIONAL DISRUPTOR

On a scale of 1-5, with 1 being the least, rate your relatability to the following statements:

_____ I can embrace failure and learn from it.

_____ I am comfortable being uncomfortable.

_____ I do not let fear impact my ability to take action.

_____ I intentionally put myself in uncomfortable situations.

How have you disrupted yourself in the past thirty days?

Fear is nothing more than feedback. It's as simple as that. However, in our modern world, that feedback is often unnecessary. Our brain is constantly scanning for threats, and it always finds something. Fear was essential for our ancestors. Even if there was a 1 percent chance the rustling in the bushes was a lion or tiger, it was practical to run. You didn't want to be the guy who assumed it was a bird or squirrel. That dude didn't make it long enough to pass along his genes.

When we find ourselves in a dangerous situation that involves the possibility of physical harm, fear can be helpful if you accurately assess the feedback and manage the risks, which can sometimes include running (or slowly backing away) when necessary. However, most of the fears we experience don't involve physical danger. In the Chapman University Survey on American Fears, public speaking is listed as number one, followed by heights and animals. Then the list gets a little weird. The last four fears in the top ten are zombies, darkness, clowns, and ghosts.

Let's unpack the fear of public speaking and heights. Unless you're speaking to a group of zombies, the fear is irrational. Your audience is made of humans like you, and let's be honest, they probably aren't paying attention. With heights, unless you plan on BASE jumping when you're looking over the top of a building, your risk of falling is negligible at best.

What's the one animal you fear the most? Sharks? They're certainly an apex predator, but how afraid of them should we be? Not very. In 2019, there were a total of sixty-four cases of unprovoked shark attacks around the world, and only five were fatal with an average of one death per year in the United States. What about humans versus sharks? On average, humans kill about one hundred million sharks per year, with most targeted by commercial fishermen for their fins and flesh. So sharks being afraid of humans is entirely rational. This enhanced fear of sharks didn't exist until the blockbuster film *Jaws*, released in 1975, told us to be afraid. What we should fear are the messages Hollywood, the media, and companies send us.[5]

Let's move on to some things you should really fear when you encounter them. First, hippos kill an average of five hundred people each year in Africa.[6] As a kid, I was taught hippos were friendly animals that liked to eat marbles, thanks to the game maker Hasbro. Second, texting while driving causes 1.6 million accidents per year, killing eleven teens *each day* according to the Insurance Institute for Highway Safety Fatality Facts. Yet somehow we convince ourselves that talking in front of a group of people is more frightening. And finally, Black Friday shopping kills an average of one person per year in the United States.[7] As an American, you have the same chances of dying by shopping on Black Friday as being killed by a shark. Merry Christmas.

Most fears are based on things outside our control. We fear failure, powerlessness, rejection, abandonment, humiliation. The list goes on. We try to control our environments to protect ourselves from these fears. In reality, we can only control three things: the thoughts we entertain, the judgments we make about them, and our choices. That's it. We can influence our environment, but you can't control it. We can't control if someone we love chooses to leave us, if a stranger humiliates us, if our boss rejects our ideas, or someone chooses to stop loving us.

Because the fear of failure is so intense, we often confuse our ability to influence with our ability to control. I do it all the time. I've become pretty good at influencing others, and when I confuse my ability to influence with my ability to control a situation, I become, you guessed it, controlling. It's not a good look, and it severely damages your ability to build strong and intimate relationships. Our fear of failure results in our risk avoidance of being vulnerable. If you are going to disrupt yourself, you must have the courage to overcome your fear of being a failure and open the door to vulnerability.

Most people have a fear of failure because they confuse failure with *being a failure*. Being a failure is giving up and not picking yourself up again. Overcoming your fear of failure starts with stepping into your failures. If you don't lean in, it's easier for it to knock you back and then down. Think about walking into the ocean. Are your chances better if you lean into that crashing wave or if you stand still as it bowls you over? Fear of failure results in walking carefully through life. How many people tiptoe to their death? If you want to be endlessly motivated, failure is vital.

> If you are going to disrupt yourself, you must have the courage to overcome your fear of being a failure and open the door to vulnerability.

Author and speaker Brené Brown is my go-to expert on vulnerability. In her book *Daring Greatly*, she describes vulnerability as **"uncertainty, risk, and emotional exposure."** It's that uncomfortable feeling we get when we step out of our comfort zone by doing something that forces us to let go of our perceived control. It's terrifying to be vulnerable. And like any fear you're going to face, it requires courage. The most important type of courage is emotional courage.

Vulnerability is what allows us to make intimate connections. Brown explains, "Vulnerability is the birthplace of love, belonging, joy, courage, empathy, and creativity. It is the source of hope, empathy, accountability, and authenticity. If we want greater clarity in our purpose or deeper and more meaningful spiritual lives, vulnerability is the path." That's what we're looking for, isn't it? If you want it, you need to learn how to control the fears that reside inside your head and be vulnerable to the external things you can't control.

What Does It Mean to Embrace Your Fears?

Embracing your fears starts with confronting your fear story. Your fear story is the narrative that keeps your fears alive. When I talk about conquering fear, I use freediving and paragliding as examples because my fear story says I'm afraid of drowning, and I'm intensely scared of heights. Maybe you fear public speaking, starting your own business, or becoming a parent. Perhaps you constantly tell yourself you're not good enough to be an artist, or you're not thin enough to run a marathon. Whatever your fear story is, identify it so you can start rewriting it.

Everyone's fears are different. Common fears include being helpless, rejected, alone, unloved, defective, inadequate, inferior, unfulfilled, and humiliated. We can all do the same two things to embrace our fears. One, we can identify them. Putting a name to fear is the first step in accepting and moving on from it. Two, we can identify what we actively do to avoid each of our fears. This place of avoidance is your comfort zone. My emotional fear is feeling defective. I overcome that by sharing my defectiveness with others until it becomes comfortable. My physical comfort zone means keeping both feet on the ground and my head literally above water. To get out of that comfort zone, I freedive (diving down as deep as you can on one breath) and paraglide (flying with a parachute looking wing over your head after running off a mountain) or do powered paragliding (launching from the ground with a fifty-pound motor and large fan on your back).

But why do I freedive and paraglide? Why not sit comfortably in my living room? Because when you're comfortable, you're not learning. You're not learning about yourself, you're not learning about your environment, and you're certainly not disrupting your status quo. When you're in your comfort zone, you're not disrupting yourself to live your best, happiest life.

While I train for both sports with some of the best professionals in the world, the threat of harm is still real, but the experience is worth it. Most people navigate through life only in a two-dimensional environment. However, when navigating in a three-dimensional environment, I've found my worries and daily problems don't exist in those moments. Only one thing exists: clarity. That clarity is precious and allows me to explore myself, even after I land on the ground.

Keisha's Story

Several years ago, I had what's called a skip-level meeting. A skip-level meeting is where you skip past the levels of leadership in your company and meet with your employees furthest out in the organization. The ones closest to the action. It was my first one, and I wanted to make sure it went well. So I prepared an icebreaker for the group. In keeping with our ShelfGenie brand, I asked, "If a Genie could grant you three wishes to do things that you could do today but haven't, what would they be?" The answers were revealing. Since the question qualified that they were things they *could* do, the reasons they hadn't done them were all fear-based. They ranged from skydiving to changing careers to ending a relationship. Since skydiving was the number-one answer for the group, I challenged the group by stating, "If everyone here agrees to go skydiving, I'll pay for it." Within a few seconds, most of the group agreed. A few holdouts finally went along with it, except for Keisha.

Keisha emphatically stated that she would *not* go skydiving … *ever*. We all knew Keisha, and her tone of voice and body language quickly convinced us that was true, and there was no changing her mind. Now I faced a difficult decision. Call off the adventure and make Keisha feel like she failed the group or make an exception, which would make her feel bad and allow for more holdouts to emerge.

From the answers that Keisha gave, I remembered her fear to face: her inability to swim. Water had been a lifelong fear. When her daughter became a teenager and began going swimming with friends, Keisha developed a competing fear, what if her daughter was in trouble in the water and Keisha could not help her? I proposed that if Keisha took her first swim lesson with us there to support her the morning of the skydiving trip, the rest could go skydiving. Twenty-seven people agreed to jump out of a plane for the first time, and one decided to swim for the first time. All of them decided to get way out of their comfort zone.

As the office manager, Keisha was the coordinator of the skydiving event and took care of the logistics and made sure everything was in order. That morning, we all gathered around the pool when she took her first swim lesson. She was terrified, but she did it. After some warm-up lessons, the instructor asked her to put her face in the water and swim a few feet to him. He slowly moved back, and when she finally came up, thinking she had failed to reach him, she turned and realized she had gone much farther than she thought. Over fifteen feet. As she continued her lesson, I quietly turned to the people next to me and announced that she was going skydiving with us today. Nobody believed me. But she did. After everyone else had jumped, she decided, very nervously, to jump. I have that jump the skydiving company did on video. Other than her screaming "I hate you, Allan!" it was a perfect jump. She smiled the entire way down. The grin on her face when she landed was worth a million bucks.

I knew Keisha was going to skydive because I saw her courage as she swam in the pool, and I know that overcoming your fear builds your courage, which lets you face another fear, which builds your courage. Courage always builds courage. Keisha went way out of her comfort zone learning to swim, and that emboldened her to go skydiving that same afternoon even though she was terrified. People often confuse people who show courage as not being vulnerable or afraid. Remember this: courage doesn't exist without fear. Ever.

Five Ways to Disrupt Your Fears

Patrick Sweeney, the Fear Guru, best-selling author, motivational speaker, and adventurer, didn't start disrupting his fears until he was thirty-five. That's right, the Fear Guru didn't start getting uncomfortable, disrupting himself, and facing his fears until he was thirty-five. When he did, his world expanded in the most remarkable ways. Here's how he tells his story.

I grew up the most frightened kid imaginable. I was bullied, and I had an abusive grandfather, so I was scared of everything. I was a kid who was sleeping with the light on in high school. That all changed in the most dramatic way when I was diagnosed with a rare form of leukemia at thirty-five. Facing my own death forced me to look back on my life, and it felt like I had wasted it, and I had had all these great opportunities given to me that I never took advantage of because of fear.

Fear of flying had always been one of my biggest fears. I saw a plane crash when I was seven years old, which created what I call my fear frontier. We all have traumatic moments when we're kids, before the age of twelve, where we start to put things in our subconscious database, and we create defense mechanisms against those specific fears. My traumatic event built what seemed like an impenetrable defense mechanism against flying.

Not being willing to disrupt my fears and fly caused me to turn down exchange programs, spring break trips, family reunions, and so many other missed experiences, all because I was petrified to fly. I always made excuses because I was so ashamed of the fact that I was scared. I mean, I had a beautiful family, and I was a successful entrepreneur wearing $10,000 suits, so to anyone on the outside looking in, I was the epitome of confidence; I wasn't afraid, I was choosing not to fly. But, if they could have seen the inside, they would see a man with almost no self-esteem.

At this point, I realized that we have a choice to make every time we feel fear; we can make a decision out of fear, or we can make a decision out of opportunity. To make a decision out of opportunity, it's always going to lead to growth, happiness, and success. But, on the other hand, if you make a decision out of fear, it always leads to regret and shame, and usually, to failure.

My forced introspection on how I was living was a life-changing lesson that took me from being the person they based the series Diary of a Wimpy Kid *on to realizing that courage was my superpower, and I was going to fly with it. My motivation, my Why, was the fact that I had people who loved me and counted on me, who needed me to be a better version of myself. I had a one-year-old daughter, and my wife was six months pregnant when I was diagnosed with leukemia, and I didn't want my daughter's memory of her dad to be a guy who was too afraid to get on the plane and take her to Disney. With that, I decided, first and foremost, I was going to get over my fear of flying.*

Once I got my immune system back, I went down to Leesburg Airport in Virginia, and I signed up for flying lessons. I skipped over the passenger role and went straight to the pilot role because I

75

knew I had to figure out how flying worked and why I was afraid of it. The first, I don't know, three or four lessons, were absolutely terrifying. Honestly, I forced myself to those initial lessons kicking, screaming, and crying the whole way—but I did it.

The amazing thing was, after those initial lessons, I started to love flying. I began to enjoy the flights and the freedom. It became one of my most significant sources of fulfillment, and happiness, and satisfaction in my life. It had been hidden away from me for thirty-five years because of fear. I became fascinated with the challenge of it and the intellectual aspects of it. I realized at that point that all our dreams are going to be on the other side of fear.

That was the jump-off point for Patrick. After that, he conquered his fear, obtained his private pilot's license, and continued to soar from there, achieving varying levels of piloting, which eventually led him to become a stunt pilot.

I've overcome my fears through knowledge and training. Looking at statistics and data and understanding what my real fear was helped me a great deal with flying. When I realized that flying in a commercial plane is one of the absolute safest things you could do, it was that kind of information that moved me to face my fears.

Facing my fears also reminds me that someday, and this is a big part of my motivation, eventually, I'm going to die. So I want to make sure that I've lived the most amazing, fulfilled life possible. I almost died fifteen years ago, and I hadn't lived life at all.

Today this Fear Guru helps thousands of people overcome their fears so that they, too, can live their dream life.

To face your fears, you must be willing to do the following:

- Get uncomfortable.

- Focus on context.

- Control your perceptions.

- Embrace failure.

Get Uncomfortable

The mental discomforts that come with freediving and paragliding have allowed me to break the physical and mental limitations I had preset for myself. The sensation that you experience underwater that makes you want to breathe is so powerful, and learning to acknowledge it without giving in to it is an incredible experience. One of the pieces of information that allowed me to excel as a freediver was when you have the urge to breathe, you're not running out of oxygen. You have plenty of it. When your body converts oxygen to carbon dioxide, even the smallest amounts can cause discomfort. Understanding that anyone can hold their breath for up to five minutes without posing any danger to themselves helped me move past the physical discomfort and psychological barriers to building up my tolerance. I confidently practiced holding my breath every chance I could. I found that relaxing, lowering my heart rate, and thinking about calm and fulfilling memories took my mind off the discomfort. My memory was walking my son as a young child on the pier in front of my parents' beach house, where I had spent my summers. Taking his hand, we walked from pole to pole looking for crabs while he asked me all the questions his intense curiosity could think of. Repeating that memory on each try allowed me to hold my breath safely on land for over two minutes.

When I arrived at my first freediving training at Dean's Blue Hole in Long Island, Bahamas, our first training event was to float in the pool with my hands on the edge and my head submerged underwater. The goal is to hold your breath for as long as you can before coming up for air. It's called the static breath-hold and is one of the freediving disciplines. On my first try, my coach, world-leading freediver Dean Chauche, stood next to me as I submerged my head in the water. As soon as my face hit the water, I played that special memory, and every time I began to get uncomfortable, I told my mind the fear wasn't real and immediately went back to watching that special movie. Finally, I began to tense up and struggle, thinking, *OK, this is it, I've got to take a breath.*

At that moment, Dean told me that if I felt like I absolutely had to take a breath, to raise my left index finger. I immediately raised my index finger, and then he calmly told me to put it down and lift my next finger. I raised my next finger. We proceeded this way until I reached my left pinky finger. At that point, I realized that I wasn't freaking out anymore. I lifted a few fingers on my right hand and then came up for air. I ended up holding my breath for three and a half minutes. I realized through that exercise the feeling you have when you start freaking out can be controlled with a mental exercise. Remember, there are only three things you can control: the thoughts we entertain, the judgments we make about them, and our choices. I found freediving was the perfect playground to sharpen those first two essential areas.

One of the reasons I love freediving is that I can take those lessons and apply them to all aspects of my life. Getting comfortable with being uncomfortable applies to all the other fears that I face in life. When paragliding, I've had similar uncomfortable experiences. Like many people, I have an extreme fear of heights. When I first ran off the side of a mountain with nothing but a harness with small strings attaching me to a nylon wing, I was terrified. My palms were sweating, my heart was racing, and my mind was terrified. However, I had spent several weeks of intense training with another world-class instructor, Zenti Bishop. My training allowed my mind to let my body jump off that mountain in South Africa. I knew the risks and had accepted the risk/reward equation by intensely training. More than a hundred hours of training and rehearsal led me to that moment. During each of those hours, there was an underlying level of discomfort imagining that moment. Every hour of training exposed me to small doses of stress in a controlled way. That's what attracted me to the sport. Flying is exhilarating and relaxing. However, everything that happens as you prepare for that moment to launch has different levels of mental discomfort.

When we choose to get uncomfortable, we open ourselves to constant learning. We learn about ourselves. We learn from others who are willing to face their fears with us. We find more inspiring peers. When we're constantly learning outside our comfort zone, we can rewrite our fear story and act with intention to continue disrupting ourselves.

> When we choose to get uncomfortable, we open ourselves to constant learning.

SAY *NO* TO COMFORT

There are two categories of no. One is a no to something new. Perhaps an opportunity is presented that is amazing, and you want to jump in with both feet. But when you probe, question, and dig a little deeper, you realize that it is not part of your vision and would deter you from the things you want to say yes to doing. So you decide to say no. That can be challenging.

The other no is more difficult. It's pushing beyond the fear of what if and saying no to complacency, no to staying in your comfort zone, no to sticking with the safe choices. It can be hard to ignore the voice that says you should take that safe job so you won't be homeless, you should stick with who and what you know so you don't risk failing, and you should keep doing what makes you feel comfortable so you don't risk humiliation. It's even harder to commit to the process of challenging your beliefs and discovering your true self that require you to ignore that comforting voice.

Joel Neeb, leadership speaker, CEO, former fighter pilot, USAF, and American Ninja Warrior contestant, knows how to say the difficult no. Joel's resume reads like the poster child for saying yes to getting out of your comfort zone and no to complacency. But when Joel received a stage 4 cancer diagnosis at the age of thirty-three, he was forced to question everything he had done in his life, and more importantly, he questioned why. That was when he discovered he hadn't said no to what made him comfortable in a long time.

My cancer diagnosis forced me to look at everything and really question everything more deliberately. I didn't have any big regrets. I didn't have anything where I said, "I just wish I could take that back." But I did regret the fact that I didn't try harder at some of the things I wanted to do in life. When I look back at those times when I didn't try, I realized that I was more interested in preserving the thought that I could do it than I was in actually trying to do it. I liked to say, "I could probably do that," more than I would have liked to have said "I tried it and I failed in the process."

That probably sounds weird coming from a guy who was a fighter pilot because you think that I obviously jumped out of my comfort zone at least once. And I did—at least once, but when I looked at where I was and why, I found that I had firmly planted myself in my comfort zone as a trainer fighter pilot. It's a mechanical skill, and it was incredibly difficult to learn. It took a long time and dedication and was very uncomfortable at first. But the truth is, I'd been coasting on it for eight years and just kind of riding that out and enjoying the accolades and respect that I got from it. I hadn't said no to the comfort level I had created for myself in a long time.

When I looked back, I remembered a moment that identified just how embedded in my comfort zone I was. I was flying probably five hundred miles an hour. I'm upside down. I'm about eight feet behind another airplane, also going five hundred miles an hour. I mean, think about when you're driving in traffic, and a car is eight feet behind you and how uncomfortable that would be, but that's just what I got used to, going five hundred miles an hour. We're both upside down, and I looked up (which was down) and I saw that there was an accident on the freeway. I thought to myself, "Ah, it's going to take forever to get home today because the traffic's going to be terrible."

I realized that I was worried about traffic as I was pulling this incredible maneuver. At first blush, you'd think, oh, that's pretty cool you're able to do that, but what had happened was it had just become rote memory for me. I was a robot doing a maneuver. There's nothing special about that.

No matter how far we push ourselves out of our current comfort zone, what we pushed ourselves to will eventually become comfortable. But as I have said throughout the book, and Joel's realization is a great example, this process is an ongoing journey, so you have to keep saying no to staying in the new comfort zones you have created for yourself.

When I was sitting in the chemo room talking about what I would do if I got healthy, I didn't say, "I'm going to go fly airplanes again for the next twenty years." Instead, I said, "I'm going to go after that next chapter of life and go be in the business world." I love flying airplanes, but I had to accept that it was one chapter in my life, and I had to say no to letting it be my life's book. I now wanted the opportunity to write new chapters.

At this point, I was fifteen years into my military sprint. Five more years and I'm guaranteed retirement, guaranteed medical care forever, guaranteed annuity. It's an attractive carrot dangling in front of me. If not for my cancer diagnosis, I might have said yes to staying with what I knew, with what was comfortable. But now I had a second chance, and I knew I had to start saying no to my status quo.

So five years before retirement, I did the unthinkable. I resigned and separated from the military and decided to go to business school and reinvent myself and do something new. It's the change, saying no to my comfort zone that feels good, not just winning in one chapter of my life.

CALCULATED RISKS

The military activated my ability to calculate risk and elevated it to a whole new level. In the early '90s, the military instituted a risk management process that rated risks into low, medium, high, and very high. By the early '90s, this was applied to all aspects of the Army, including training exercises. Military training exercises have their own inherent danger such as shooting live artillery rounds or conducting air assault missions using helicopters to lift our artillery and equipment behind enemy lines to get better range. My job as a young lieutenant was to assess the risks, rate them, mitigate them, and re-rate them. If there was anything above a certain level after the risk mitigation was completed, we had to sign off from our battalion commander or division commander. Going through this process for every exercise we did in the field increased my competence at risk assessment and my understanding that most risks, especially physical risks, can be mitigated.

To conquer your fears, you must calculate the risk. Once you identify the risks, it's easy to mitigate them. Both Patrick and I are constantly looking for ways to grow through fear. Most of that growth doesn't come in the action. Instead, it happens when training, rehearsing, and mitigating each level of risk in our minds. For me, holding my breath and experiencing the calm of free falling over a hundred feet into the darkness of the ocean or flying a thousand feet in the air with a wing over my head and an occasional eagle flying beside me is worth the risk. It creates large doses of mental discomfort that stretch and push our imagination. It builds strong defenses to stress and makes us more prepared when we confront real-life problems. It creates resilience by giving us context and the clarity to understand it.

In addition to calculating the risk, one must also commit to accepting the risk.

Do I accept the risk? That is a question Matthias Giraud, world record–holding big mountain skier and BASE jumper, asks himself when setting his next goal and before each jump. If the answer is yes, he helps his loved ones understand his quest. *When you help your loved ones understand why you are willing to take the risk, it enables you to commit to your goal.*

Commitment is no stranger to Matthias. In 2013, Matthias suffered a double fracture of his femur, and a brain hemorrhage after his jump went seriously wrong. He body-slammed the mountain four times on his descent, fell four thousand feet unconscious, and crash-landed in a forest, falling another fifty feet onto the dirt.

While rehabbing, I continued to envision myself BASE jumping. I also came to realize there was meaning to be found in my failure. First, it was a test of my dedication. It wasn't only about accepting the risk but also asking, "Do I have what it takes?" I knew I had to return to the basics and retrain to build my foundation because clearly, I wasn't as good as I thought I was. I also knew I needed to be a solid dad to my son, born just three weeks after my accident. An essential part of being a solid dad was continuing to self-actualize and reach my goals and objectives as an individual.

Six years after the accident, Matthias climbed the summit of Mont Blanc with forty-five pounds of gear and ski BASE jumped from the summit, closing the Alps trilogy—Eiger, Matterhorn, and Mont Blanc—and setting a world record in the process.

Before the accident, while climbing to the summit, I would be 80 percent committed to jumping. Now I wait until I am at the top and can assess all the real-time variables and risks before I make the decision to jump. Today my commitment to jumping as I begin my ascent is always fifty-fifty.

With the maturity of perspective, I have also learned to take the time to digest my accomplishments and to spend time at home enjoying family and friends before setting my next goal.

Focus on Context (Your Bad Would Be Someone's Best)

Context is powerful. It's what creates gratitude. If you learn to look at your experiences through the lens of context, you can grow. Context is a strong foundation when dealing with fear. As an entrepreneur, whenever I get stuck in a fear loop, my go-to thought is "At least I'm not being shot at." When I deployed to the Middle East in 2005, I had a healthy fear of being killed every time I went outside of the wire. In those environments, that fear is what helps keep you alive. As the Civil Affairs Section (C9) Battle Captain and later OPSO (Operations Officer) for the Coalition Land Component Command (CFLCC) covering Iraq, Afghanistan, and the Horn of Africa, our mission was unique. We would work to win the hearts and minds of the local population. All our missions were conducted in civilian clothes without the visible presence of a weapon.

Each time we'd go outside the wire, there was a real chance our vehicle would be rigged to explode every time we left it out of sight. When we'd get back to our vehicle, we'd spend thirty minutes checking it before starting it. Even after a thorough inspection, starting it was terrifying. Since the chance of us being taken hostage was high, we went through hours of training, not only to avoid it but to learn what we should do if it happened. Going through that training and recalling it while in the field was uncomfortable but necessary to reduce the risks. It also created context when I got home. It was surprising to realize the fear-based mental discomfort in my entrepreneurial world before my deployment often matched and sometimes *exceeded* what I experienced while deployed. That context always helps me reset my fears in a safe, comfortable environment. I could also look at my family, who I was separated from for six months, and instantly feel gratitude that washed away whatever leadership fears I was experiencing at the moment.

You don't have to go to a combat zone or jump off a mountain to create context. While my son, Paige, was growing up, I intentionally took him to third-world countries for relief and mission work. He was in Haiti several times when he was six and eight years old, visiting an orphanage we supported. He went to the Dominican Republic when he was twelve to visit villages Hope International supported through microfinance. On those and other trips, we'd always come back with a strong appreciation for all we had. It also built some of the best memories. You can't help but notice how people in some of the most difficult circumstances are happy. They sing, smile, and show love and appreciation for the people around them.

While they live in adversity almost every moment, they don't experience the type of anxiety most of us do every day. That's why practicing deliberate adversity can be a helpful tool. If you think your life is difficult, make it even more so. Psychologists refer to this as desensitization. It lowers your emotional responsiveness to a negative after you are repeatedly exposed to it. We take our comforts and possessions for granted, and even still, we pursue more. Deliberate adversity gives you context. Context gives you the gift of gratitude. Gratitude motivates you to help people. Helping people gives you the gift of happiness and makes stress and anxiety melt away during those moments. There is an ancient Chinese proverb that says,

If you want happiness for an hour, take a nap.

If you want happiness for a day, go fishing.

If you want happiness for a month, get married.

If you want happiness for a year, inherit a fortune.

If you want happiness for a lifetime, help somebody else.

Control Your Perceptions

When you control your perceptions, you live in the present. When you fail to control your perceptions, you live in one of two places where you can't truly exist—the past or the future. Guess what else lives in the past and the future. Fear. Fear lives in the past as regret and in the future as anxiety. When you learn to control your perceptions and live in the present, you escape fear. Learn to control your perceptions by

- intentionally directing your actions,

- accepting what's outside your control, and

- avoiding extreme reactions before they occur.

INTENTIONALLY DIRECT YOUR ACTIONS

Studies have shown that a problem must be addressed in a matter of seconds, or the likelihood of resolution significantly diminishes. Controlling your perceptions means mindfully directing the actions you want to take the moment you want to take them. It doesn't mean waiting until January 1, 2025, or January 1, 2045, or January 1, 2060, to make a change. It means doing it now.

Intentionally directing your actions also means not letting *past* actions dictate *future* actions. When something negative happens to us, it becomes a part of our fear story. This story, like a fear of heights for me, dictates our future actions. Our brains do this to protect us; however, just because I may have fallen off the monkey bars when I was six doesn't mean I need to let that story dictate how I approach heights for the rest of my life. When we cling to past fear stories, we narrow our perception of what's possible *today*. Therefore, when you're directing your actions, make sure that your actions are not taken based on an old fear story. Instead, take action based on the facts of what's happening here and now. Take action based on a *calculated* risk.

ACCEPT WHAT'S OUTSIDE YOUR CONTROL

Take a second and think about what makes you anxious. Are you worried about how you'll pay for your kids' college *in ten years*? Are you afraid that you might lose your job *someday*? Are you obsessing over that presentation you have to give *tomorrow*? The great thing about anxiety is that it primarily generates from worrying about *future* events or things that are utterly out of our control. Yes, you can take some actions that might help these future situations, but why worry about the rest once they're taken? You can set up a savings account for your kids, work to meet your goals, and practice your key points for the presentation, but *there's nothing you can do about the future* outside those specific actions. Once you've taken the actions available to you, every other worry about the future is pointless. Intentional disruptors understand that there are only certain pieces of life that they can influence, so they focus on those actions and let everything else go.

AVOID EXTREME REACTIONS BEFORE THEY OCCUR

Fear directs us to think in extremes because it forces us to look for the worst-case scenario in any situation. Our fear stories can trigger extreme reactions. However, suppose we take control of our perceived notions of how a future event will emotionally impact us. In that case, we can avoid creating an unrealistic fear narrative that prevents us from making fact-based decisions. We need to employ what psychologists refer to as a psychological immune system that protects us from experiencing extreme negative emotions long term.

Studies have shown that humans are poor predictors of how intensely and for how long they will feel emotions connected to a future event. We typically create an imaginary narrative that says we will feel good or bad about an experience far longer and with more intensity than that feeling will be in real time. This means that too often, we are making decisions based on what we imagine or perceive. The intensity and longevity of our emotions will be at the conclusion of an experience.

> We have the power to hold no opinion about a thing
> and to not let it upset our state of mind—for things
> have no natural power to shape our judgments.
> —MARCUS AURELIUS

How we perceive our reactions and emotions to a future experience negatively impacts our ability to make decisions in our own best interest. "We underestimate how quickly our feelings are going to change in part because we underestimate our ability to change them," concludes Harvard University social psychologist Daniel Gilbert, PhD. "This can lead us to make decisions that don't maximize our potential for satisfaction."[8]

This doesn't mean that we will never experience intense emotions, but we can adjust our perceptions to create more rational expectations of those emotions. Controlling those perceptions before an experience will also aid in moving past negative emotions once they do occur.

THE POWER OF PERCEPTIONS

At my franchise conferences, I always want to build on the positive perceptions of the franchise owners. I do that in the context of what we learn from failures, how we overcome failures, and how we build upon those failures.

Years ago, at one of ShelfGenie's annual franchise conferences, we arranged to kick off the conference's second day with a couple of hugely positive stories. We lined up a couple of franchisees with great customer interactions and success stories about how things went wrong and how they turned it into a positive experience for the customer. We were all pumped about the positive energy this would create. The first presenter got up on the stage, looking a little weary from the social event the evening before. Behind him was a giant slide, "Success Stories with Matt Davis," and Matt started telling this harrowing customer story, and everybody was waiting for the success moment, but it never came—it was a disaster story to the end. Because Matt happened to be off his game that morning, he defaulted focusing on the negatives of the story. Then he launched into other disasters with customers that he never brought to a resolution. He also never talked about anything he learned from those failures.

The next speaker got up to tell his success story, and what did he do? He followed the cycle Matt had started and told his own disaster story with the obvious goal of outdoing Matt. The mentality changed from the intended success stories to "Oh, you think that one's bad, mine's worse." It terrified all the new franchisees. That fear-based cycle is easy to fall into if we're not careful. Controlling your perceptions and nurturing a growth mindset can help you break that cycle.

Embrace Failure

At the most painful moment of any failure, you're incredibly powerful. It's almost impossible to tell at that point, but as you look back, it's easy to see the power we all have to disrupt and reinvent ourselves endlessly. That's why failure is productive. It's the most powerful way to learn about who you are and how you can become a better version of yourself.

We can't talk about conquering your fears without addressing one of our society's biggest fears: the fear of failure. University of California Professor Martin Covington conducted a study that shows a fear of failure is directly linked to our self-worth.[9] We pride ourselves on being good at x, y, or z, so when we fail at x, y, or z, it feels like an attack against our self-worth. But that's only if we negatively attach ourselves to failure. Professor Covington says, "By making our self-worth contingent on categories such as academic success, appearance, or popularity, we fail to value ourselves solely for the fact that we are human beings and accept that failure is part of the human experience." Welcoming failure opens the door to self-worth. She further explains that if people think they may fail or have repeatedly failed, they will seek to preserve their self-worth through practices that take the form of excuses and blaming.

Here's the funny thing: if you want to succeed, you must first fail. It's true. A person is unable to predict what action would be successful without first learning what actions are not successful. Learning from our misses, failures, whatever you want to call them, updates our expectations and strategies for our next attempt. According to neuroscientist Dr. Dafna Shohamy, our brains assimilate information for the purpose of prediction.[10] The ability to predict the consequences of our behavior is one of the primary goals of our brains. For example, when you touch the stove as a child, you experience what is known as a *prediction error*, which, according to Dr. Shohamy, is a learning signal to update your expectations for the next time. So if you want a lifetime of growth and success, be open to experiencing a never-ending stream of prediction errors.

I learned to start accepting failure after experiencing a frustrating loss in business. In 2005, I decided to sell PuraTech, the air filtration company I started in 2003. PuraTech was growing fast, and profits were soaring. Annual sales were at about $1.3 million, and our sales close rate was excellent. Then unexpectedly, I received a notice that I would have to deploy, so I decided to sell the business. At first, there were several interested buyers. That is, until they took a closer look. Of the $1.3 million in sales we had, I had personally generated more than $900,000. I had a 78 percent close rate, which was great, but our next best salesperson had a 40 percent close rate. In addition to these discrepancies, we also had a turnover rate of about 300 percent. Well, it didn't take long for my prospective buyers to realize that based on the current projections and business model, things would take a severe dive as soon as I left. Someone finally offered to buy it, but they didn't want to pay any money up front. Instead, they offered to give me an earn-out based on profits. I was running out of time and didn't have any other option, so I took it. Five months later, PuraTech was out of business. Not only did I not receive any profits, but I also watched a company I'd started and grown fail. When you get to the office every day at 6:00 a.m. and are still working by midnight so that you can grow a business that ultimately fails, it's painful.

What is productive failure? PuraTech was a painful failure for me. I experienced depression over its loss and had to adjust my thought process as to who I was. When you spend over a year working eighteen-hour days building a company, it becomes your identity, and so in addition to the shutdown of the business, I felt like I lost part of myself. Who was I without a company that I worked for so many hours each day?

As I gained time and perspective from the PuraTech experience and assessed what had gone wrong, I knew I needed to make PuraTech's failure productive. I used what I learned from my mistakes to build my next business, ShelfGenie, successfully. One of the first things I did was make sure I wasn't a salesperson for the company. If I had learned one thing from PuraTech, it was that all aspects of the business could not depend solely on me. I put together a process to recruit, train, and mentor salespeople and build on that. I also knew I needed to eliminate the high turnover rate that plagued PuraTech. We utilized independent contractors paid based on performance rather than hiring installers on salary. In the end, I took what was an excruciatingly painful lesson and turned it into a productive failure that enabled me to build a multitude of companies that generated over $50 million in revenue annually.

I also developed an exit plan, which was something I hadn't done before. When someone starts a business, how to exit the business is usually the last thing they consider. Whenever I interviewed potential franchisees, I would ask them what their exit plan was, and most of the time, there'd be a long silence. Having a good exit plan defines what both success and failure look like so that you clearly establish, if certain things happen, it's time to stop. That was the biggest lesson I learned; it's easy to define success and very hard to define failure when planning. Who wants to think about failure when planning something new and exciting? If you don't determine what failure looks like, you can't define success.

One of my failures in business was a company that was very profitable the day it closed. We lost our biggest customer, and after several months of trying to fill that gap, it was clear we weren't going to get there before we ran out of money. We failed fast and closed the company down with cash in the bank. We didn't make that decision lightly. We did it after carefully watching the data and financial projections of the company.

> If you don't determine what failure looks like, you can't define success.

Failures in business usually occur within the business, not to the business. However, the same principles apply. In my companies, every team member knows that they're not doing their job if they aren't failing. Sometimes I'll let the team know that we're not failing enough and push them to fail more. We can do this because we have the safety net of assessing the risks and knowing how to fail fast in advance.

If you're going to fail, you need to be able to fail fast to mitigate your losses.

When embraced, failure can:

- inspire you. When the act of failure doesn't define you, the outcomes from it can inspire a new thought, project, or approach to the problem.

- teach you humility. Failure is always a humbling experience, but this isn't a bad thing. It simply reinforces that you are, in fact, human. Everyone fails.

- allow you to take more risks. Surviving failure reinforces your resilience, and when failure is accepted as a part of growth, this resilience will encourage you to take more risks.

- make you have a better appreciation for success.

- be your greatest teacher. If you are willing to accept failure and think about it not as an adverse event but as a way to receive feedback, you can learn great lessons from failure that may very well lead you to success.

None of us aims to fail on our way to success, but we're human. We will fail. Why not fail quickly, embrace the failure, and move on to better, brighter things?

Facing your fears is uncomfortable, painful even, but once you learn to do it, there's nothing you can't disrupt. Fear is the number one emotion that holds us back from becoming our best selves. Once you get comfortable with fear, face it head-on, and rewrite your fear story, you'll be amazed at how little control it has over you or your future. Failure *is* an option, and I hope you receive it as a gift when it presents itself.

Takeaways

- Fear is nothing more than feedback.

- Most fears are based on things outside our control.

- Your fear story is the narrative that keeps your fears alive.

- When you're comfortable, you're not learning.

- The feeling you have when you start freaking out can be controlled with practice.

- When you control your perceptions, you live in the present.

- Controlling your perceptions means mindfully directing the actions you want to take the moment you want to take them.

- Controlling your perceptions and nurturing a growth mindset can help you break your fear cycle.

- You need to define success *and* failure.

Action Items

- Identify two of your biggest fears. Putting a name to fear is the first step in accepting and moving on from it.

- Now identify what you actively do to avoid each of those fears. How does this avoidance impact your life?

- Identify the fear story you have been carrying around. Unpack it, assess it, and write a plan to move past it.

CHAPTER 4

Observe Your Impossible

Possible things aren't worth much, it's those crazy
impossible things that keep us passionate and alive.
—BOB BEAUDINE, *THE POWER OF WHO*

STATEMENTS OF AN INTENTIONAL DISRUPTOR

On a scale of 1-5, with 1 being the least, rate your relatability to the following statements:

_____ I am comfortable in chaotic situations and can handle ambiguity.

_____ I am curious about what's happening around me and spend significant time observing.

_____ I often dream about possibilities and practice being creative.

_____ I have an optimistic attitude, especially in difficult situations.

Has your intentional self-disruption begun to disrupt those around you?

The military provides a lot of value to many people because it teaches discipline and structure. As I mentioned in chapter 1, it helped me figure out who I am, what I value, and what I want to do with my life. As I was getting ready to graduate college, I was given orders for active duty. I reported to Fort Sill, Oklahoma, to complete my Officer Basic Course. I loved the training, but Fort Sill was a lesson in the not-so-glamourous training grounds of the military. Fort Sill is a barren, desolate landscape, and the town itself had nothing to do. It was an hour's drive to get to Oklahoma City and three hours to Dallas, Texas.

As I was finishing up at Fort Sill in the winter of 1993–94, we were asked to choose a first, second, and third choice for our permanent station of duty. I knew there was better than Fort Sill (no offense to Oklahoma). Winter in Fort Sill starts around October. The bone-chilling wind was the absolute worst, especially when we had to get up at 5:00 a.m. for physical training and were forced outside in shorts and a T-shirt. Although we were warmer in the classroom, it was pretty miserable there too.

I quickly learned that one of the most coveted Army bases was in the Schofield Barracks in Hawaii. I desperately wanted to go to Hawaii, and so did almost every other lieutenant in the Army finishing their training. We knew we could list Hawaii as our first choice, but other than that, we were told the selection process was out of our hands. Getting one of the coveted slots in Hawaii was about as likely as winning the lottery.

Getting to Hawaii was a long shot, a long shot if you were willing to submit your request, sit back, and hope for the best. I'm not a sit-back-and-hope-for-the-best kind of person. I wanted to get to Hawaii and knew that if I didn't do something, I never would. So I started asking around. No one seemed to know. First, I found out who chose the assignments. There was some captain buried in the depths of the

Pentagon who was responsible for assigning artillery officers. I combed through several military Defense Switched Network phone books (yes, phone books were still the go-to in 1994), found his phone number, and called it. Of course, to get to the captain, I had to get through his assistant, which required a little persuasion. I told her my plan and found out she loved Hawaii and missed the local macadamia nuts from her vacation there. Instantly, we reached a deal. If she'd let me talk to him and I was successful, I'd send her a box of them.

When she put me through to him, I was pretty blunt with my request. "Sir, I put down Hawaii as my first choice of assignment, and I'd very much like to get it." Getting straight to the point is the preferred method of communicating in the military. He was quiet for what seemed like minutes but was actually a few seconds and then said, "Well, I have five slots for Hawaii and over four hundred artillery lieutenants to assign. Since I have to assign everyone before they finish their training, there isn't an order of merit [long pause]. No one's called me before, so sure, you can go to Hawaii." And it was as easy as that. I went to Hawaii, and for the first time in my military career, I started observing how even in an organization where the group comes before the individual, there are opportunities to influence and do things outside the box.

Getting my first assignment in Hawaii was one of those pinnacle moments in life that dictated so much of the rest of it. I started my military career in Hawaii, which introduced a business opportunity that eventually led me to start my first business. So many incredible things happened in my life as a result because I was curious about possibilities and made a phone call no one else had even tried to make.

I ended up in Hawaii, living on one of the most beautiful beaches in the world in front of the Pipeline surf break because I observed my depressing physical environment, questioned the status quo, decided I didn't like what my future looked like, and acted.

What Does It Mean to Observe the Impossible and Question Everything?

In 2004, Nobel Prize winner in economics Daniel Kahneman set out to determine what makes people happy.[11] He started his study by interviewing people about their workdays. Specifically, he asked each of his subjects to explain everything they did during the day and then categorize each episode as a like or dislike. Then he looked at parents and discovered that, on the whole, parenting is a rather miserable experience. If you think about the day-to-day activities of parenting—changing diapers, wiping noses, cooking meals, cleaning up after the kids, shuttling them to events, playing referee—there's very little reward. Yet Kahneman found that the parents he interviewed viewed their children as their greatest source of happiness. The question had to be asked: do humans simply not know what makes them happy?

Not necessarily. While we're led to believe that happiness can be measured in pleasant and unpleasant experiences, that's not necessarily the case. Instead, happiness is measured by how we *perceive* our lives. When we perceive our lives as worthwhile and meaningful, we're happy. When we *perceive* our lives as a waste of time and pointless, we're unhappy. The common denominator here is *perception*. From a nonparent standpoint, parenting looks miserable, yet the people doing

> When we perceive our lives as worthwhile and meaningful, we're happy. When we *perceive* our lives as a waste of time and pointless, we're unhappy.

the miserable work love it because they *perceive* it to be worthwhile. As Kahneman demonstrated, our perceptions form our reality. And how do we develop our perceptions of the world around us? Through questioning and observation.

When you make a point to observe and question, your perception of the world will change. You will see things you missed before, and you will begin questioning things that you've never considered before. This practice will open doors you previously thought were closed, and it will lead you to that place where life is meaningful.

Five Ways to Observe Your Impossible

To engage the left side of your brain so that you can observe the impossible and question everything, you must:

1. Have the right attitude.

2. Embrace ambiguity and chaos.

3. Question everything.

4. Unfocus.

5. Pay it forward.

HAVE THE RIGHT ATTITUDE

Think about your day yesterday. How much control did you *actually* have? Did you order the weather you experienced? Did you choose to go to work, or did you go because you need to pay the bills? Did you ask that Starbucks barista to spill your double latte on your laptop bag, or did it just happen? Did you know your son would give you a drawing, or did he surprise you with it? If you're honest, your answers to these questions should prove how little control you have over any of your days. As much as we want control over every little aspect of life because control makes us feel safe, it just isn't possible. There are only three things each of us can control: the thoughts we entertain, the judgments we make about them, and our choices. If you're Disruptable, you control thoughts and feelings in four very specific ways.

If you're Disruptable, you:

- remain positive,

- confront confirmation bias and fudge factor thinking,

- are indifferent, and

- reframe adversity.

Remain Positive

Is your glass half empty or half full? Research repeatedly indicates that those with half-full glasses live longer, produce greater results, enjoy life more, experience less stress, and are happier than pessimists.[12] If you want to be your best self, if you're going to be Disruptable, you have to commit to being an optimist.

Typically, when something goes wrong, people become very pessimistic. They tend to play the blame game, which is driven by fear. "Who did this to me? Whose fault is this?" On the other hand, an optimistic person will take a longer-term view of the problem at hand. They'll look at the failures, they'll figure out what went wrong, and then they'll learn from that situation regardless of who was in the wrong so that they can move forward.

Confront Confirmation Bias and Fudge Factor Thinking

Confirmation bias is, at its core, wishful thinking. Wishful thinking reinforces the ideas we have about ourselves and our surroundings as we'd like them to be, not as they are. When we fall into a pattern of wishful thinking, we can't possibly observe and challenge everything because instead of seeking the ideas and people who will challenge our perceptions, we sit safely with our ingrained beliefs.

Most people have confirmation bias because of an ideology. For many of us, our ideologies are formed from beliefs ingrained in us since we were kids. The problem with ideologies is that they're never correct 100 percent of the time. For a lighthearted example, let's compare Coca-Cola and Pepsi. When I was a kid growing up in Virginia, everyone I knew drank Coca-Cola. My family and I rarely saw anyone drinking a Pepsi. When we did, we would think, *What is wrong with them?* We actually had an ideology behind who drank which kind of soda and grouped people according to that belief. This concept is applied to much more serious situations, such as politics and religion, and the lesson is that we need to question our beliefs and why we believe them. No one ideology is correct all the time. If you're Disruptable, you're ideology averse, allowing you to form your own thoughts and feelings and *change* them as you learn and grow.

Challenging your beliefs is a conscious decision that Ken Stern, former CEO of NPR, made in 2016. Ken spent a year with conservatives. Coming from a liberal ideology, Stern wanted to see if the information he was getting about conservatives from the media was correct. Were conservatives as bad as some media made them out to be? His answer? Not at all. In fact, Stern found that spending time with people who shot guns and ascribed to religious beliefs far from his uncovered commonalities rather than differences he thought he had with conservatives. This example and other stories are reflected in the title of the book Stern published as a result of this experience, *Republican Like Me: How I Left the Liberal Bubble and Learned to Love the Right*. Stern's experiment proves that challenging your belief systems can bridge the gaps that you thought existed between you and others. Challenging your beliefs is a lesson in growth.

Fudge factors are in the same category as confirmation bias. Fudge factor thinking occurs when people use common rationalizations to justify bad behavior. One of the most widely recognized examples of fudge factor thinking involved Harvard primate psychologist Marc Hauser.[13] Hauser spent hours and hours watching videos of his monkeys (which is what a researcher is supposed to do). However, when Hauser was alone with the monkeys, he "observed" and recorded behaviors that none of his lab assistants ever saw. Although false, these behaviors supported what Hauser hypothesized the monkeys would do. Eventually, one of Hauser's lab assistants blew the whistle on Hauser's questionable scientific process, and Hauser became the center of a media circus.

Confirmation bias and fudge factors keep us living in a world full of inaccuracies. If you want to change, if you're going to excel at anything, you have to be able to truly observe reality.

If you're Disruptable, you observe the world as it is, not as you wish it would be.

Are Indifferent

Indifference is most powerful when it's applied to drama, negativity, and negative people. Using indifference to disengage from those negative situations allows you to go and focus on positive people and places that will help you grow. Practicing indifference in these situations is practicing a growth mindset rather than a fixed mindset.

> If you're Disruptable, you observe the world as it is, not as you wish it would be.

By suggesting that intentional disruptors are indifferent, I don't mean that we're apathetic. Let me be clear: intentional disruptors are indifferent about things that *don't matter*. While they are open to input and ideas from others, they ignore 99 percent of the advice they are given because they understand that while most people mean well when giving advice, the advice-giver rarely understands the receiver's goals, values, or desires.

People aren't upset by events. Instead, they're upset by their judgment of events. If after an accident the doctor tells you that you might not regain the feeling in your legs, feeling pain is a good sign. Did you get fired and end up getting a better job? Then getting fired was good. What happens to you isn't good or bad. It's your interpretation of those events that's good or bad. This Chinese proverb illustrates the point:

> A farmer and his son had a beloved stallion who helped the family earn a living. Then, one day, the horse ran away, and their neighbors exclaimed, "Your horse ran away. What terrible luck!" The farmer replied, "Maybe so, maybe not. We'll see."
>
> A few days later the horse returned home, leading a few wild mares back to the farm as well. The neighbors shouted out, "Your horse has returned and brought several horses home with him. What great luck!" and the farmer replied, "Maybe so, maybe not. We'll see."
>
> Later that week, the farmer's son was trying to break one of the mares, and she threw him to the ground, breaking his leg. The villagers cried, "Your son broke his leg. What terrible luck!" The farmer replied, "Maybe so, maybe not. We'll see."
>
> A few weeks later, soldiers from the national Army marched through town, recruiting all the able-bodied young men for the Army. "Your boy is spared. What tremendous luck!" to which the farmer replied, "Maybe so, maybe not. We'll see.

Reframe Adversity

Domino's Pizza is a technology company that happens to sell pizzas, and Amazon is a technology company that happens to sell a bunch of stuff. Today every successful company is a technology company that happens to sell pizza, books, or, in ShelfGenie's case, custom shelving for cabinets.

For the first few years, we used a technology company's technology platform to manage every interaction with our customers. Then as we grew, we decided to rebuild that system with a company that allowed us to own the code to protect our intellectual property better.

The development of that new system was under the control of my new IT director. It felt good to have someone else manage that, but as it was being developed, I had a feeling that things were going just a little too well. I've been involved in many software implementations, and the days leading up to going live with a new system are hectic. Yet the days leading up to launching this new system were very calm. Too calm.

At launch, everyone was happy and smiling. Then over the next few days, the cracks started to emerge. Massive cracks. It didn't work. For the next six months, every technology integration that ran our company before either didn't work or didn't work very well. It was excruciating for everybody involved. It was painful for me as a leader because I had to take full accountability for the massive mess. Fortunately, our selling system was on a different platform, so all our locations could keep selling. However, our operations and ability to complete jobs for our customers came to a grinding halt.

We brought in a team of six people from our developer to work on the system. I worked alongside them for over six months, seven days a week with some days that ended after midnight and started back up at 6:00 a.m. It was an absolute nightmare. Still, throughout that process, I reminded our team about other times when things broke down entirely and how these breakdowns are a natural process for any fast-growing company. I'd often use a house remodeling analogy and explain that while we were living and sleeping in a house as it was completely rebuilt from its framing, we were ultimately going to end up in an amazingly remodeled, better version of our house. It helped take the edge off the crisis but not the pain. One franchisee told me, "I know at the end of this, you'll end up making this way better than where we were before. I've seen it happen each time something in our process breaks as we outgrow it. But for now, I'm going to hate you."

I believe a leader's number one job is to reframe adversity. They need to refrain from making the fear-based knee-jerk reactions we all want to make when something goes wrong. They're responsible for seeing the lesson in the mistake and communicating it frequently and often. When done correctly, people will see what lies on the other side of the storm and work through it with you, but don't expect them always to be happy about it.

Leaders can reframe adversity by preparing for adversity. They look at every situation, assess it, and think, *What could go wrong?* That way, when that something does go wrong, they're not knocked off balance. Because they're not knocked off balance, they can learn from the situation and react to it rationally. And when you don't see it coming, like the example above, you must be the one seeing the long game and lead everyone through it, happy or not. I remind myself in those situations by asking two questions: If not you, then who? If not now, then when?

For the next few years, if you were considering purchasing a ShelfGenie franchise and came to a Discovery Day at our headquarters, you'd hear me tell that story. And several others like it. I only told stories to prospective franchisees about our failures. Why? Because the results of those failures were astounding to share. After the technology system debacle, our system sales and profits were more than double the growth of any other year in our history. When leading an entrepreneurial company, I know that we learn, grow, and do better every time something goes horribly wrong. If you learn to reframe adversity, you'll inspire yourself and those around you.

EMBRACE AMBIGUITY AND CHAOS

Many people love routine and predictability. It makes them feel safe. It keeps them from putting themselves out there and facing possible rejection, which makes them feel in control. But the reasons people cling to routine and predictability reside in the fixed mindset zone. People with growth mindsets understand that they must learn to embrace ambiguity and chaos. There are two reasons for this. One, they accept that ambiguity and chaos are a part of life. As I shared previously, there's simply no way to control anything except your thoughts, feelings, and actions. Two, they understand that if they don't embrace ambiguity and chaos, they'll never try anything new because what is a new experience but unpredictable? If you're in an unpredictable situation, chaos is present, if only in your mind.

Embracing ambiguity and confusion doesn't mean you throw yourself into total chaos; it means you have to be willing to let go of control and routine. Think of it as "organized chaos." I first heard this term when I was a fire direction officer in the military. My section sergeant had a sign in our fire control center that simply said, "Organized Chaos." He would use that term to describe to our team what it's like in battle. Going into battle requires you to be disruptive and create chaos but, more importantly, respond to the chaos created when the enemy doesn't follow your plan. (They never do.) When you plan for chaos, you can quickly adjust when it presents itself.

Set Your Own Rules

To me, life is one big game, a puzzle to be solved. When you view everything in life as a game, it's not only fun, but you get to set your own rules. Remember when you'd play a new game as a kid? You wouldn't read the instructions or rules. Instead, you made them up as you went along and had *fun*. It's only as we get older that rules are introduced into games and problems emerge.

Games without rules are creative and fluid. When you view problems as a game, you can set your own rules on how to play with them. Too often, we're presented with problems and both written and unwritten rules on how to solve them. More importantly, the rules define the problem. Question the rules about problems when you're presented with them. While the stakes may seem high and the possible results seem catastrophic, remember that you can question the options and predicted outcomes. "Losing" the game may be the best option even though no one around you sees it. I'm highly competitive, but I often question the rules of what's considered a win. Walking away is sometimes the best way to win, while others see it as a loss.

Nothing is permanent, although most problems present themselves this way. The people around you set that rule when framing the problem and decide what's a win or a loss. The fact that they don't see it as a game or that they're setting the rules for the game is to your advantage. Play the game as you did as a child. Consider your own rules and definition of winning. You don't have to always play by the rules of others.

When you embrace that nothing is permanent, you can do almost anything you want because you stop trying to hold on to everything. How often have you outgrown what you once thought you couldn't live without and, soon after, fall in love with something you didn't even know you wanted? That comes from society setting the rules.

You always need something bigger and better. And if you don't get the next big thing, you have a problem. The challenge of living by other's rules about problems is they are constantly changing. So why not set your own rules of what's a win and what's a loss? The game is all in our heads. As Maya Angelou said, "If you don't like something, change it. If you can't change it, change your attitude."

QUESTION EVERYTHING

I grew up questioning everything. Part of it was because I was a kid, and kids naturally question everything. I also had this innate desire to know how everything worked and why it worked that way. Being Disruptable means constantly challenging the way you perceive the world.

Kofi Smith, at the early age of seventeen, dared to question a well-laid path to his future. Scholarship to one of the top medical schools—check. Opportunity to quarterback for a Division One team—check. With all the stars aligned, Kofi asked, "But what about …" That questioning mindset in combination with the right attitude and an openness to perceive the world through differing lenses led him to become President and CEO of the Atlanta Airlines Terminal Company at Hartsfield-Jackson Atlanta International Airport.

I was offered a full scholarship to Vanderbilt, which included playing quarterback for a Division I school alongside my friend Eric Wissman, who was going to be my tight end. We were a package deal. Michael Passarella, one of my best friends in high school, and I both had plans of becoming orthopedic surgeons and setting up practice together. Vanderbilt, a top medical school, was the key to my future self. When the time came to commit, I began questioning my choice, and I'm blessed that my mom and dad gave me complete autonomy to question my options and to make the decision on which school I would play football for and get my education.

I was a shy boy from Alabama who wanted to play football and be a doctor. As an African American playing quarterback in high school in the 1990s, I looked for college quarterbacks who were African American to emulate—we didn't have a lot of Black quarterbacks playing Division I football or playing in the NFL at that time. Georgia Tech had Sean Jones, and I was a huge fan. I wore my wristbands like Sean Jones, the same face mask, you name it. That was the only thing I knew about Georgia Tech when I applied. I was accepted. It wasn't a medical school, and they weren't offering me quarterback. They were offering me defensive back. Vanderbilt kept coming up as the obvious answer to where I should go, but I felt compelled to find out more about Georgia Tech.

When I visited Georgia Tech, I was blown away by the city, the skyline. I was blown away by the scale of it all and by all the beautiful women that seemed to be everywhere. There was nothing on my future plan's checklist that fit with Georgia Tech, but I decided to follow my gut, and I signed on as a Yellow Jacket. By the end of my freshman year, I began to question my future as a doctor. Georgia Tech is the number one industrial engineering school in the U.S., and I decided that I needed to take advantage of the opportunity before me, and I set my sites on becoming an industrial engineer.

Kofi's questioning of the status quo and the benefits of not taking the easy path didn't end there. His first job out of college was in a manufacturing plant.

After my acceptance, my plant manager asked me, "Do you want to be an industrial engineer, stay behind a table, and run cost analysis, time studies, and financials, or do you want to get on the manufacturing floor and have a team report to you?" I told him that I wanted the team. He smiled and said, "I was hoping you were going to say that. I'm going to give you the worst team. They have the lowest productivity and process reliability. I'm giving you the worst team because you're either going to sink or swim."

I observed the team and quickly realized that they were good people. They were just in the wrong position. I continued to question the process and look at things differently. I got to know everyone and build up trust. Then I helped everyone find their sweet spot on the floor. Within six months, we were the number one shift within the company. We broke records, set records, and people started to notice.

Kofi's capacity to observe, assess, and see things in new ways have led him to break many records. When Kofi accepted the position of CEO for AATC, he found his footing by asking questions not only of himself but also of those he intended to lead.

The first thing I did at AATC was interview all forty-three employees. I wanted to understand the good, the bad, and the ugly of the organization, and so I asked a lot of questions of each individual beginning with what did they want to see from me and what did they not want to see from me. I shared my leadership approach with each of them, compiled all the information, and then presented it to the leadership. It was important that I honored the people's trust by executing that process. The people I lead come first, my shareholders come second, and customers are third. I believe that if I don't take care of the people that I lead, there's no way I can take care of my shareholders or my customers.

Kofi's ability to disrupt the status quo and see new ways of doing business has led to his most recent success: leading Hartsfield-Jackson Atlanta International Airport to become the first airport in the Western Hemisphere to achieve ISO 55001 certification.

UNFOCUS

This may sound counterintuitive to everything you heard from teachers growing up, but taking time to *unfocus* can ignite your mind. Harvard researchers have found that the default mode network (DMN) circuit in our brain, informally referred to as the "do mostly nothing" part of the brain, actually does a lot.[14] When this circuit is at rest, it uses 20 percent of the body's energy. This is impressive considering that any other effort requires only 5 percent of the body's energy. So what does the DMN do? It dips into the subconscious, races to the future, returns to the past over and over, combining ideas from all three along the way. This is how the brain prepares ideas for the conscious mind to examine.

This brainwork is part of the unconscious mind, and to come up with new ideas, problem solve in creative ways, and unleash creativity and new ideas, the DMN has to be allowed to work. While teachers may tell us to hurry up, stop daydreaming, and focus (if I had a dollar for every time I heard those statements directed at me), if we truly want to excel, we have to practice the art of unfocusing.

Meditation is an effective way of unfocusing. Although I still struggle with sitting still for thirty minutes, meditation allows me to keep my mind from wandering. When your mind isn't focusing on anything, creativity follows. This is how you begin to break away from the pack. Take some time every day to sit still and do *nothing*. Ironically, by taking some time to stop your constant mind-racing problem-solving, you end up solving many problems … often by gaining the perspective that most of them are not problems.

PAY IT FORWARD

Ralph Waldo Emerson once said, "The purpose of life is not to be happy. It is to be useful, to be honorable, to be compassionate, to have it make some difference that you have lived and lived well."[15]

Doing things for others and being selfless activates the same pleasure part of your brain that sex and food do.[16] When this part of the brain is activated, we naturally feel more pleasure, which opens us to other positive emotions that, in turn, feed the way we view our world.

In 2005, I decided to spend some time volunteering. After my deployment to the Middle East, I got involved with a micro-finance nonprofit, Hope International. I spent time in Haiti and the Dominican Republic helping people start small businesses so they could feed their families. I remember being in the Dominican Republic in a sugarcane field while visiting the small Haitian communities that had been given microloans of about $50 to start businesses. These migrant workers came to the Dominican Republic, sometimes illegally, and were paid about $1 a day to work in the sugar fields. They were impoverished. Some of them didn't even have clothing.

The group we supported had set up their businesses in the middle of a sugarcane field. There was a concrete building with about ten stalls in the middle of the field, abandoned by the company they used to work for years ago. As I walked around and spoke to them, I learned about their new businesses. One lady sold refined sugar, another sold fried chicken, another had a sewing machine that she used to make and mend clothes. Finally, reaching the end of the stalls, a lady was standing outside on the corner of the building. I asked her about her business. She smiled from ear to ear and said, "I have a gas station."

I thought she was joking. After all, she had that huge smile. She obviously saw my confusion and said, "Come with me." Behind the stalls, she had lined up Coke bottles filled with gasoline. She then told me, "I sell gasoline to the people on the small motorbikes that go on the road that don't live in our community," as she nodded to the dirt road that went by where we were standing. I smiled back as I finally understood. Then she taught me something I didn't grasp until much later. "What you have to understand," she said, "is if we only sell to each other, we don't bring any resources, any money in from the outside. And if we don't sell to other people and buy from other people, then we don't get any better." I was blown away. She explained micro and macroeconomics to me in a way that most people with four-year degrees can't.

Whenever I return from situations like this, I am first over-whelmed by a feeling of gratitude. I'm also in awe of how much I learn and how happy the people are with their lives, despite having far less than any of us do. Engaging in selfless acts reinforces what's meaningful and where true happiness lies. I always learn much more from these experiences than I do from our environment, where we have everything we could need and much more than we should ever want. Being selfless is a gift to yourself more than it's a gift to others. Be selfishly selfless whenever you have the opportunity.

Takeaways

- Happiness is measured by how we *perceive* our lives.

- If you want to be your best self, if you want to be Disruptable, you must commit to being an optimist.

- Intentional disruptors are indifferent about things that *don't matter*.

- Leaders reframe adversity by preparing for adversity.

- Embracing ambiguity and confusion means you must be willing to let go of some control and routine.

- Nothing is permanent, although most problems present themselves this way.

- Being Disruptable means constantly challenging the way you perceive the world.

- Taking time to *unfocus* can ignite your mind.

- Engaging in selfless acts reinforces what's truly meaningful and where true happiness lies.

Action Items

- Take a day to observe and question your thoughts and how you interact with the world around you. What things did you see that you had never noticed before?

- Take time every day to sit still and do *nothing*. Then write down any new ideas that came to you during your time of unfocusing.

- Make a plan of how you can pay it forward over the next twelve months.

CHAPTER 5

Act Intentionally

You miss 100 percent of the shots you don't take.

—WAYNE GRETZKY

STATEMENTS OF AN INTENTIONAL DISRUPTOR

On a scale of 1–5, with 1 being the least, rate your relatability to the following statements:

_____ I am resilient when I face setbacks.

_____ I gravitate toward mentally difficult situations.

_____ I do not expect instant gratification.

_____ I communicate my vision clearly and continuously.

Now go back and add up all your responses to the previous quizzes to see how you track against the max score of 100. I recommend taking the quiz, which is summarized at the end of the book, every three months. Are you continuing your journey to break away from normal by embracing your fears, observing the impossible, and acting intentionally?

Dan Lok, entrepreneur, best-selling author, philanthropist, and business strategist, knows how to act. Like me, Dan had to act and fail, act and fail, act and fail before he discovered the value of acting intentionally. Like me, Dan was a young entrepreneur and had thirteen failed businesses by the age of twenty-one. But he knew, even if it meant more failures, he had to keep taking action and had to pay off his business debts and make a living for his family. He also knew he couldn't do that on a minimum wage job that his limited education would provide—he would have to dig deep.

When I was seventeen years old, my mom and dad got divorced, and then my dad went bankrupt. He was living in Hong Kong, and my mom and I were living in Canada. So as the only child, I had to grow up fast and provide for my family. A Chinese immigrant new to the country and the language, I was always thinking of ways to make money. I mowed lawns, I made deliveries, I fixed computers, I owned a vending machine business. None of that worked. I had thirteen failed businesses between the age of seventeen and twenty-one. Today people say, everything I touch turns to gold. Back then, nothing I touched turned to gold.

Looking back, I can laugh, but at the time, it was very difficult. I wasn't doing well in school, and my mom was worried, and I was just this crazy young entrepreneur that had all these ideas, but none of them worked. I lost all my mom's money in that period—everything—and we had borrowed money from different relatives and her friends to fund all my business ideas, and we ended up losing that too. So it was a very challenging period, but I wouldn't be where I am today without those failures.

I knew I eventually had to make it work. It could be the four-teenth, fifteenth, twentieth business. It didn't really matter. I had to make it work. What kept me going back then was a belief I held as I observed other people who didn't work as hard as me or weren't smarter than me make their business successful, so I had that belief that I'll work and I'll learn, and I'll figure this out. And eventually, I did.

The shift for me came when I found a mentor, Alan Jacques, and I learned from him how a business works, how you get customers, how you grow something, how you make sales. And that was a shift for me, and that kept me going.

I worked for Alan for one year for next to nothing. People would say to me, "You're stupid. Why would you not get paid? Why would you not demand more?" I would tell them that I didn't care about that. And it was true. Yes, financially, it was a real struggle, but I wasn't working to make money. I was working to learn. I knew I needed to learn a skill set, and Alan taught me the skill of copywriting and how to market it.

From there, I started my own one-man advertising agency. Working from home, I was in my early twenties, and I was writing copy for entrepreneurs and businesses. In that one-man agency, I was able to generate $10K a month. I was thrilled that I was able to provide for my family and slowly pay off those debts. I kept learning and expanding my skill set, which prepared me for the opportunity the internet presented around 1995. That's when I "made it," thanks to the trend, thanks to the internet, thanks to my having the skill set when the opportunity presented itself.

I am always open to opportunities. I recognize when I see something special, and then I put more effort into it. Perfect example, when I started accessing YouTube a few years ago, I never thought it would be where it is today. The first video I uploaded was just a transfer because the video of my speaking presentation was too large. But then people started showing interest in it, and I started getting calls. I thought, here's something very special, and then I put serious effort into it. It took us two years to go from zero to ten thousand subscribers on YouTube. Then to go from ten thousand to one hundred thousand subscribers only took one year. From one hundred thousand to one million took us another year. So in two years, we went from ten thousand to one million. That's a one hundred times growth. I could see the opportunity, and then I went all in, stayed focused, and kept going.

I am also all about learning from others' mistakes; I read about others' failures and best practices and learn from them. My first business failed because I let my ego get in the way. I didn't have a plan, just an idea. I started the business and thought only of its success. I was overconfident and overly optimistic, and most entrepreneurs are like that. The other reason they failed is that I was trying to do everything on my own. It was when I connected with Alan J. that I learned how businesses actually work. He taught me many things like how to fail, write copy, and get customers. And I realized, OK, I had all these great ideas for products and services, but I had no idea how to actually get it in front of people to sell the product. That was the answer for me, a mentor. It may not be the answer for everybody, but that was the answer for me.

What Does It Mean to Act Intentionally?

Acting intentionally means taking control of your life before someone or something else does. It means understanding that those who do not act are always *acted upon*. When you're reacting, you're being acted upon. When you're proactive, you're acting. You're developing a plan, observing who you are, deciding, and setting yourself up for whatever greatness you want to achieve.

In *The Power of Moments: Why Certain Experiences Have Extraordinary Impact* by Chip and Dan Heath, the authors explain what happens to "peak experiences" as we move through the decades.[17] Peak experiences are typically defined as transformational learning experiences. Most of these altering events occur in a person's teens and twenties. By the time we're thirty, they begin to taper off. By the time we hit forty, they're nearly nonexistent.

It's not that we can't physically, spiritually, or emotionally have more peak experiences as we age. It's that, as we age, we move from a growth mindset to a fixed mindset. This happens for numerous reasons, the primary one being that we stop growing to conform to social constructs.

When you commit to having a growth mindset, you can create these peak experiences for yourself throughout your lifetime. But doing this requires both commitment *and* action. So whether you start acting by confronting your fears, orienting yourself, or getting out of your comfort zone, the idea behind *intentional disruption* is to help you rewire your thoughts and motivations. This allows you to take the right actions to put your life on the track *you* envision for it.

Six Ways to Act Intentionally

To ensure that you act before you're acted upon, try the following:

1. Move with velocity.

2. Do what's hard.

3. Channel your grit and resilience.

4. Unlearn instant gratification.

5. Trust but verify.

6. Communicate your vision clearly and continuously.

MOVE WITH VELOCITY

When we first started ShelfGenie in 2005, we didn't have instant success. Many days I thought, *Why am I doing this? It's the worst thing ever.* Then as we continued to grow the business, I would think, *Why am I doing this?* one day, and the next I would think, *This is amazing.* The highs and lows were all over the place.

After our first year in business, my business partner said, "Things are always crazy. We're moving way too fast. We're making a lot of mistakes." But I firmly believed the only thing keeping us together was the velocity that we were moving at. I felt like we were our own plane. Things weren't necessarily screwed on correctly, but the main thing that was keeping the parts on the plane was the fact that we're moving so quickly. Because we had a clear destination of where we wanted to be as a company, we could move rapidly in that direction and keep the parts on the plane together. That's what velocity does. Velocity is speed and direction. When you move at high speed in the right direction toward your vision or your goal, that's what holds it all together when things get ugly.

DO WHAT'S HARD

We've talked about hard things such as confronting your fears and getting out of your comfort zone for a reason. If you want to become your best you, doing the hard stuff is nonnegotiable. Most things are hard because they're mentally hard, not physically hard. We always give up mentally way before we meet our physical limitations.

Whenever I have a hard time getting through something difficult, I think about another time where I did something hard and succeeded. This always helps me get over that hump. You can also think about other people who have done hard things and use them as inspiration. I'm constantly reading about people who have found great success by doing what's hard. Getting through the hard stuff requires grit and determination.

One of my inspirations comes from my son, Paige. Very early on, he loved doing hard things. After a few years of car camping, he became interested in backpacking. When he was seven, while on vacation visiting family, we went to a small backpacking store in the North Georgia mountains. The owner helped outfit us with backpacks and all we would need to fill them and hike into the unknown. We had lots of fun planning for that first trip—getting all our gear together, choosing the food we would take, and planning out the route.

Our first trip was to the Shenandoah Wilderness Park in Virginia. Our plan was to start at the top of the mountain where the trail began and hike down the trail about three miles to the bottom where there was a backcountry camping spot on the map. We made it there just before dark, set up our campsite, cooked dinner, and settled into our new tent and sleeping bags. The next morning, we woke up and made a spectacular breakfast.

As we were eating, Paige and I started reviewing the map of the trail I brought with me so he could learn about map reading. He saw a large loop going around the park and asked why we weren't following the loop. I told him that it was a twelve-mile loop, and going around the loop was nine miles, three times farther than we went the previous day, and it was up and down several mountains. He wanted to do it, and I explained it would take all day. He got very excited and insisted we try.

At that moment, I knew he was asking to do something hard, but he couldn't grasp how hard it was. I decided to let him try. Worst case, we'd spend another night camping with a bit of leftover food. Over the next eleven hours, we hiked up and down those mountains. About halfway into it, it started to rain. Shortly after, he decided this was a bad idea. He was cold, wet, and utterly exhausted. I explained that to get back to the car, we'd have to keep going in the same direction since we'd passed the halfway mark of the twelve-mile loop. For the next six hours, I motivated him to keep going with words of encouragement, silly songs, and a gummy bear every time we completed thirty minutes of walking. Each gummy bear represented an accomplishment. We'd take a break, eat one slowly, and laugh about how much it sucked. That's when I taught him the phrase I learned in the Army: "Embrace the suck." He thought it was hilarious. Probably because it was the first "bad" word he was allowed to say.

It made the rest of the trip more bearable. When he would get tired and close to our planned thirty-minute gummy bear break, he or I would exclaim, "Embrace the suck!" the other would laugh, and then we'd laugh together. He was so exhausted that I carried his pack the last half mile as he struggled to get up the last bit of the mountain to our car. As we were getting into the car, I'll never forget that smile on his face as he laughed and said, "Daddy, we sure did embrace that suck!" and then he fell fast asleep.

As hard as that first backpacking trip was, he was all in for doing more. We'd do several each year for the next eleven years of his life.

Each year, as he grew stronger and his pack weighed more, I found myself having to keep him in check so he wouldn't push his little body too far. Eleven years later, it's still one of our favorite activities together. Spending days away from electronics and distractions, alone in the woods, just the two of us, became a special time that created a strong bond and connection between us. The fact that sometimes it sucked made it even more special for us.

When Paige was fifteen, we decided to go on an extreme adventure. Jesse Itzler's, author of *Living with a SEAL: 31 Days Training with the Toughest Man on the Planet*, experience living with famed Navy SEAL David Goggins sparked this crazy question: what if we had a group of 150 people attempt to climb an insanely steep mountain repeatedly to equal the height of Mount Everest in under thirty-six hours? That question led to the endurance challenge 29029. If you're wondering, the event's name is the height of Mount Everest in feet.

After several months of training for the 29029 event, Paige and I found ourselves at the base of Stratton Mountain in Vermont. At precisely 3:00 p.m., Paige and I began our adventure up that mountain along with 148 others. Many of them were ultramarathoners, triathletes, and experienced climbers. Paige was one of two kids and the youngest. After an hour of climbing over a mile and 1,800 feet of elevation, we reached the top of the mountain. After the climb, we took the gondola down with the other participants. At the bottom of the gondola, you're faced with two choices: turn around and climb again or take a break and enjoy a massage and a sampling of gourmet meals from five-star chefs. We chose the former and went up again.

As the day turned to night, we completed three ascents. Each time I went a little slower. Each time I was a little more exhausted. Paige was like a jackrabbit. He would always be ahead of me, resting a bit and waiting for me to catch up. Soon after sunset, the weather turned, and the gondola was closed for safety reasons, and vehicles were sent to the top to give participants a ride down a steep dirt road that was rough, to say the least. I decided to call it, and we had a great meal and a good night's sleep.

We woke up at sunrise and began climbing again. Paige started climbing with me and a group of friends who were extreme athletes. Among them was Daley Ervin, an ultramarathoner who had just rowed across the Atlantic Ocean, and another who had climbed all of the seven summits, including Everest. About twenty minutes up, Daley was beginning to have extreme leg cramps, and Paige offered to go back down the mountain and retrieve some potassium supplements that could help. He caught up with us about thirty minutes later with a big smile and the promised aid. A little later, the others began to climb faster than me, and I could tell he wanted to go with them.

I told him to go with them, and he said, "Dad, I want to stay with you. This is *our* adventure." I had a thought that came out of my mouth before I could process it. I told him that my job raising him was to help him become a man who would someday be able to go faster and farther than me. He asked several times if I was sure, and each time, I assured him that it was OK. He smiled and quickly climbed to catch up with them. While my heart slightly broke as I watched him go without me, the rest of it was filled with pride and joy.

Two-thirds the way up on his next ascent, his body broke down, and it took him another hour to complete the last third of the climb. I was waiting for him at the bottom as he emerged from the gondola. We got some food, and he lay down in the tent completely exhausted. For most people, that would have been the end of the day, but not Paige. Several hours later, he rallied and insisted on doing more climbs that day. It was now clear there wasn't enough time to complete all seventeen ascents.

I asked if he was sure, and he responded, "Dad, I want to complete as many ascents as I possibly can." As we began again, each step for him was an exercise in pure grit and determination. He was no longer the fastest. His body was broken, but his spirit was not. I encouraged him as he pushed himself further than he thought his body was capable. He climbed the mountain eleven times in total—the height of Mount Kilimanjaro in under forty-eight hours. Only a few completed seventeen climbs and many less than eleven ascents.

Most people in the group not only learned his name, but they also learned his story as they would walk with him for a bit on his slow climbs up that Saturday afternoon. Even more powerful, their stories of why *they* were doing this crazy adventure inspired him to continue pushing on. As we celebrated with everyone at the end of the event, I saw a different person than I knew before that adventure. One who was more confident in his capabilities and potential.

CHANNEL YOUR GRIT AND RESILIENCE

As defined by psychologist Angela Lee Duckworth, grit is living life like a marathon and not a sprint.[18] It's one's passion and perseverance for long-term goals. It's sticking with your future day in and day out for years. It turns out that grit is a significant predictor of success, often irrespective of a person's IQ or talents. Duckworth and her team conducted research with West Point Military Academy cadets, National Spelling Bee participants, rookie teachers working in challenging communities, and salespeople in private companies to see if they could predict who would succeed in those groups and who would not. In each of those different contexts, one characteristic emerged as a significant predictor of success. It wasn't social intelligence, good looks, physical health, or even IQ. It was grit.

When you envision your future, set goals to achieve that vision, and stick with those goals day in and day out for as long as it takes, you will significantly increase your chances of success. Working in tandem with your passion and perseverance toward reaching a long-term goal is the resilience to continue bouncing back from inevitable setbacks.

> *More than education, more than experience, more than training, a person's level of resilience will determine who succeeds and who fails. That's true in the cancer ward, it's true in the Olympics, and it's true in the boardroom.*
> —DEAN BECKER, PRESIDENT AND CEO OF
> ADAPTIV LEARNING SYSTEMS

Diane Coutu, director of client communications at Banyan Family Business Advisors, observed that almost all the theories on resiliency she researched shared three core components.[19] Resilient people embody a staunch acceptance of reality (while a healthy dose of optimism is required, to be resilient, we must also be able to accept the harsh reality that life is not a bed of roses), a deep belief in a life with purpose, and an uncanny ability to make do with what they have when situations go south. Diane suggests that two or three of these traits will enable most of us to bounce back from hardship, but all three are necessary to be truly resilient.

UNLEARN INSTANT GRATIFICATION

In the 1960s and 1970s, Stanford researchers tested children's impulse control to see what effect patience had on long-term results.[20] They gave the children a marshmallow and told them that they would be rewarded with a second marshmallow if they could resist eating their marshmallow until the researchers returned. Then the researchers left the kids alone for fifteen minutes. Later in life, the researchers returned to the same children (now adults) and looked at their successes. Interestingly, the kids who passed on the instant gratification of one marshmallow to receive the second marshmallow did significantly better in achieving long-term goals than those who immediately satisfied their sugar craving.

When anyone starts a new company, the positive results are always in the future. It's hard work for years and years with the goal to sell the company one day with a big payoff. One of the determinations I made up front with ShelfGenie was to take our profits and reinvest them into the company. I did this to increase the value of the company and accelerate its growth. Investing profits back into a company year after year doesn't lead to instant gratification. Instant gratification is taking those profits and spending them. If you want to intentionally disrupt your life, you must actively decide not to seek instant gratification.

We live in a world of Amazon and Uber Eats, so it's even more challenging to deny instant gratification than it was years ago. Whenever my son wanted to buy something with his own money, I had him wait three days. If he still wanted to buy it after three days, he could. Interestingly, he rarely wanted to buy the item after getting over that initial yearning for instant gratification.

TRUST BUT VERIFY

When I was a lieutenant in the Army, I always had additional duties, and one of these duties was to watch over all the vehicles. I had a motor sergeant working for me full time. He was in charge of overseeing the maintenance of these vehicles. Every Monday he was supposed to go through a checklist on every vehicle. Then once a month, he was supposed to go through a different, more detailed checklist for each vehicle.

One of the weekly items was taking the air filter out of each Humvee and inspecting it. I don't know if you've ever had to do this, but accessing a Humvee air filter is time-consuming and frustrating. It is not as simple as popping the hood and pulling out the air filter. It requires a lot of unhooking and putting back together of parts. As a result, many of the guys skipped this step.

I knew that we were trusting these guys to check the air filters on the Humvees, but no one was verifying that the soldiers had, in fact, inspected them each week. So I decided to go to the motor pool early one morning before the guys arrived. At the end of the day at formation, I asked, "Raise your hand if you inspected the air filter on your Humvee this morning." Everyone raised their hand. Then after a bit of planned silence, I looked at Private Jones and asked, "Where's my note?"

This private had no idea what I was talking about. He didn't know that around four thirty that morning, I had written a note asking him to come see me and left it inside that hard-to-get-to air filter of his Humvee. I proved my point. The private received several small but well-deserved consequences, and the rest of the guys started checking their air filters each week as we started doing random inspections regularly.

If you're going to act intentionally, you must be able to fail fast and move forward. This means that you have to delegate some of your tasks. You're going to have to trust people, but trusting someone isn't enough. In addition to trusting them, you also have to verify that they're doing what they said they would do.

COMMUNICATE YOUR VISION CLEARLY AND CONTINUOUSLY

Quantum mechanics Nobel Prize winner Richard Feynman famously said, "I think I can safely say that nobody understands quantum mechanics."[21]

How can a Nobel Prize winner say he doesn't understand quantum mechanics when the world has recognized him as a leader in that field? Feynman's explanation was that the only way

> If you're going to act intentionally, you must be able to fail fast and move forward.

a person can understand anything is if they can explain it in simple terms. If you cannot explain your vision to yourself first and then to others in simple terms that are universally understood, you don't know what you want.

I remember when the topic of the importance of communicating your vision came up in discussion with a group of CEOs. I learned that I wasn't communicating mine very well. One of the CEOs stood and said, "Most of the time as leaders, what we have in our head is not communicated to everybody in the organization and the people we're leading. Most of the time, we think it is because we're saying certain things, and they're saying, 'I got it,' but they don't know what they don't know. They don't truly know what we are envisioning. It's not a vivid vision."

Then he shared an example of when he called someone to the front of the room to explain his vision. He told the participant that he wanted to plan a party and that there should be music. He wasn't sure what kind of music he wanted, just that it needed to be fun. He wanted it to be an outdoor event in a lovely natural setting. He wanted it to be a lunch event, a really nice lunch served outside. The music should go with that setting, and it should be music that people can sing along with.

Now he asked the participant to describe how he would create that event, what it would include. The response was "Well, we'll have karaoke, it'll be outdoors, we'll have a nice buffet table set up where everybody can have lunch, and it'll be in a nice park."

Then he pulled up a slide, which was a picture of *The Sound of Music* in the big open mountain field, and they're playing guitar and singing together with a picnic lunch spread out before them, and he said in a well-faked frustrated tone, "That's what I wanted, and you didn't give me what I wanted." Everyone laughed as they understood the difficulty of communicating a vision and why things often go wrong for leaders when they don't communicate their vision in great detail.

I learned that it takes a whole lot more than repeating a general description to communicate a vision. I also realized that a majority of my job as a leader in an organization is communicating vision and culture and making sure that I'm saying that vision over and over.

Communicating your vision is a very repetitive process. When I think about communicating a vision, I often think about golf. Golf is a challenging game to learn. It takes years of constant trying and modifications to get better, and the only way to get better is to keep your eye on the ball. It also takes repetition, lots of repetition. The same is true for communicating your vision. When you share your vision with others, you will say it repeatedly year after year until you achieve it. I know I'm communicating my vision enough when I see people roll their eyes when they hear it. But I think leaders need to constantly recommunicate that vision. I have a group of people who I consider my personal board of advisors. After I've repeated my vision over and over to the leadership team and employees, I go to my board to check in. Am I keeping my eye on my vision? It's essential to surround yourself with accountability partners. The more people you tell about your vision, the more likely you are to achieve it.

Takeaways

- Acting intentionally means taking control of your life before someone or something else does.

- If you want to intentionally disrupt your life, you must actively decide not to pursue instant gratification—positive results take time to create.

- Grit is a significant predictor of success that requires sticking with your future day in and day out for as long as it takes.

- To act intentionally, you must be willing to fail fast and move forward.

- It's essential to communicate your vision and surround yourself with accountability partners.

Action Items

- Gather two or three inspiring peers and ask them to hold you accountable for your newest idea/vision after explaining it to them in detail.

- Make a list of the lifelong pursuits that you are willing to stick with day in and day out, no matter how hard it gets.

- Make a list of people who inspire you and why. How are you alike? How are you different?

- Take your crayon vision drawing from chapter 2 and share it with the people you want on your journey with you. Communicate what it means to you and your plan to make it happen.

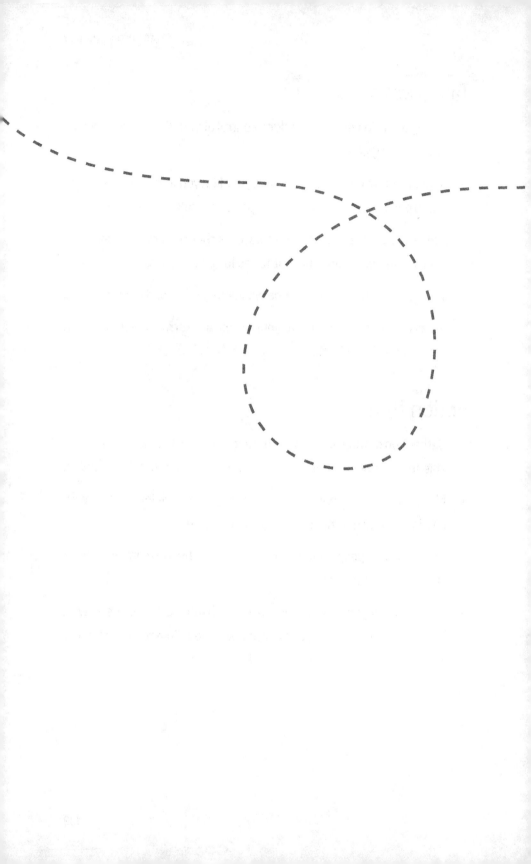

CONCLUSION

Flying twenty-five miles per hour at one hundred feet, I began my descent and prepared to land my paraglider. Suddenly, I felt the wind shift and my wing catch on something, abruptly turning me toward a row of power lines. I had a decision to make. Hit the power lines that were one hundred feet in front of me or immediately collapse my wing and plummet to the ground to avoid them. I made the decision with the time I was given. In less than a second, I pulled my brakes hard, collapsing the wing of my paraglider and crashing myself to the asphalt below. As I dropped, I instinctively tucked my legs, pulled my elbows into my sides with my arms bent, looked forward, and tried my best to keep my body relaxed. Successful emergency landing. Many may debate me on calling my crash landing a success, but for me, it's all about controlling my perceptions.

What did my successful crash landing look like? I couldn't walk away from it, but I was alive and still conscious.

After impact, the first thing I noticed was that my forearms were scraped, and then I realized I was still strapped into my motor. The mangled heap of metal was leaking gasoline all over me. I knew I needed to get up and get this thing off me quickly. It took a heartbeat for me to realize why I couldn't get up. I couldn't feel or move my legs. My first thought at that moment was *I might not be able to paraglide again.* It may sound strange, but when you have a consuming passion that brings you tremendous joy, its loss feels greater than other potential ramifications. My following thoughts were trying to process and solve for a life where I might not walk again. Then the shock from the landing wore off, and my body exploded with pain.

This wasn't how I had envisioned the start of our annual visit with my family in Colonial Beach, Virginia, unfolding. The previous year's visit, I had been able to paraglide along the beach and Potomac River. Flying over the beach where I was a summer lifeguard in high school, the river and bays where I had water-skied almost daily, and the areas where I used to take my rowboat to check my crab pots filled me with so many happy memories. On September 29, 2020, I woke up looking forward to a replay of last year's flight, but life doesn't always follow our plan. I didn't know it then, but I would have months to unpack why my plan went so horribly wrong and how I would continue to move forward.

My son had been the first to arrive at my side that day, yelling for onlookers to call 911. As he ran up, he asked if I was OK. My response was slower than normal. "Yeah ... I can't feel my legs." It was an unsettling forty-five minutes before the ambulance arrived. I did my best to appease my son's and the gathering crowd's concern, telling them that I would be fine and back to paragliding soon. Unfortunately, it didn't have the desired effect. Especially with my mom, who arrived with the rest of my family members a few minutes later. Instead, it added concern about how hard I might have hit my head.

Eventually, the ambulance arrived, and they rushed me to the hospital in my hometown of Fredericksburg. During the ride, I was injected multiple times with pain medicine. In the movies, those injections cause immediate relief. Unfortunately, it wasn't working out that way for me. After the third injection, the paramedic finally told me that if she injected me with any more, my heart might stop. She explained that because the pain was so intense, my body was instantly burning off the medicine. I tried to negotiate a minor heart attack for another injection, but she wasn't having it. I did manage to make her laugh most of the trip there, which was more for me than her.

Shortly after arriving at Mary Washington Hospital, my luck began to change. The neurosurgeon on call that afternoon was from Walter Reed Hospital and was one of the top neurosurgeons in the world for traumatic spine injuries. After reviewing my X-rays and MRI, he told me my L1 was fractured, and my L2 was burst, and he had a good plan going into surgery. As he spoke, the room grew dim, and my next memory was waking up in a hospital room alone. A nurse came in shortly afterward and let me know I had been in surgery for over six hours and that it was now after midnight. She asked me if I needed anything. I asked for a phone, and I did what any man would do in that situation. I called my mom. When she answered the phone after the first ring, I told her I was fine and not to worry. I don't think those words helped her at that moment, but they helped me.

Before I could doze off again, the doctor arrived for the moment of truth. "Move your toes for me." All the toes on my right foot wiggled freely, but on my left foot, only my big toe would cooperate. "OK. Lift your legs for me." My right leg followed orders; my left leg wouldn't budge. A few seconds of silence and I blurted out, "Will I be able to walk again?" I knew better than to ask that question and immediately saw by the doctor's reaction that he had expected me to. It wasn't a no. Instead, it was a well-rehearsed response: "Maybe. We'll see. It's going to take some time." Not what I was looking for. As I pushed for something more definitive and rephrased my question using every sales technique I had ever learned, I received several rounds of equally matched evasive answers. "The spinal cord and nerve damage is complex," "The human body can sometimes surprise us," and my personal favorite, "You're lucky to be alive." This guy was good.

I was in the hospital for two weeks until I could be transported to the airport to fly home in a wheelchair. During those two weeks, I was only allowed one visitor because of COVID-19 restrictions. My mom visited every day, sneaking in my favorite ice cream from the local favorite Carl's Frozen Custard, along with cookies and other treats she made each day. While I was in pain, I looked forward to the time I spent with my loving mother. She encouraged me through the beginning of my physical therapy.

Despite my left leg atrophying to a third of its original size, I was able to walk with my back brace and a walker around the hospital ward after the first day. My left leg wouldn't work, but the therapist showed me how to use forward momentum, lock my knee, and take another step with my good leg. Before long, I ditched the walker and was able to take careful, slow steps. My nurse encouraged me to walk as much as possible, and I took her up on that offer, walking laps around the ward for hours each day. She finally told me that our definitions of "as much as possible" were very different. I responded by asking, "Is that going to be a problem?" She laughed and said, "That won't be a problem, but I can see that you're going to be one."

Between PT sessions and visits from my mom, I was able to get some work done. With COVID-19 raging, I joined conference calls with my companies and boards, sold one of my companies, and bought another. But there were still many hours left in the day and night to fill and only my thoughts to fill them—this idle time pushed me out of my comfort zone more than adjusting to my physical limitations had. Breaking my back forced me to slow down and simply be in the moment. If you've ever tried to sit quietly with no distractions for hours on end during a traumatic event, it's mentally painful and uncomfortable. But after a few days, I learned to be comfortable with that discomfort and use it as a weapon to change my mindset.

After days with seemingly no progress and excruciating pain, I called my friend Matthias Giraud, the world-famous BASE jumper. He and I were paragliding together in the mountains of Tennessee the week before my accident. We spoke about the sport's inherent danger and our *Why* behind our passion between flights. He had already heard about the accident, and we got straight to the point of my call. How do I recover my strength from a leg that had massive nerve damage and had atrophied to a third of its original size?

I told him about the multiple "maybes" the doctor gave me about walking again and returning to normal. Having broken many bones in his body, including his femur, and then climbing Mont Blanc less than a year later to ski and BASE jump off it, he was my go-to expert on recovery. He laughed a bit and said doctors have one question they must answer definitively: "Is everything technically correct with my body?" He said if the answer was yes, I'd make a full recovery. I immediately called my doctor, and after a slight pause, he answered my question with the response I was looking for: "Yes, your spine has been corrected, but the nerve damage is extensive and may never grow back."

Before I began to mount a full recovery, I needed to do a painful assessment of my landing. I had to access my ignorance, embrace my fears, and embrace failure. The truth was unavoidable. Although I was able to make the split-second decision that saved my life, the crash was caused by multiple pilot errors. Without those mistakes, the entire catastrophe would have been avoided. In Malcolm Gladwell's book *Outliers*, he said, "The typical plane crash involves seven consecutive human errors." I counted three, but my errors happened moments before landing.

First, I changed my flight plan. My original plan was to fly over the tree and land further down the beach. However, as I made my approach, I decided to go to the right of the tree to land closer to where I took off, making the walk back to my car with the fifty-pound motor easier. Sometimes you need to change your plan if conditions change. In this case, I chose to divert from my solid plan out of pure convenience.

Second, as I began to prepare for my landing at about one hundred feet, I focused intently on where I wanted to land and lost all situational awareness. In the military world, it's called target fixation. You focus so intently on the target that your vision is like looking through a straw. As a result, you're not seeing what's happening around you in the moment.

Finally, I was thinking about where I wanted to go instead of where I should go. Before I began my flight, I had a clear vision of my entire flight. I envisioned my takeoff, flight, and landing. In the pilot world, it's called chair flying. The principle applies to anything you do in life. Vividly visualizing how you're going to successfully do something increases your chance of success. When you change that original vision for extraneous reasons, your chances drop significantly, and you don't achieve your vision. That's the definition of failure.

Armed with this information, I could now confidently lay out a path to move forward. Six months after the accident, I visited my surgeon, and he took me through the battery of strength tests for each leg. I showed him not only could I walk using both legs, but my left leg had also gained over 50 percent strength of my right one. He told me I was a walking miracle. Something he assured me he reserved for only a few of his trauma patients over his thirty-year practice. On that day, he told me he had no doubt I would make a full recovery. A month later, I went freediving and made a near-personal best of 102 feet. On Father's Day, nine months after the crash, I completed an eight-mile backpacking trip with my son in the mountains of North Georgia with thirty pounds on my back. While every section of the book applied to how I handled my crash, here are some examples of how I used the principles of *Disruptable* in my successful recovery.

FIND YOUR *WHY*

I knew exactly my *Why* for wanting to recover. It wasn't to do basic tasks in life. I wanted to freedive again. I wanted to go on challenging backpacking trips with my son again. I desperately wanted to get back to pushing my physical and mental limits to rediscover the peace away from anxiety and stress that I only find when I am out of my comfort zone. When you have bipolar disorder and live with higher-than-average levels of mental discomfort, activities that allow you to unfocus become necessary treatments. I needed the comfort that I can only find from being uncomfortable. For me, stress and anxiety can't live in those spaces.

All other results from walking and finally running again were added benefits. When you find experiences in life that provide you mental relief and immense happiness, you're willing to do almost anything to get back to it. During the many hours I spent on my recovery, I would keep a clear picture in my mind of doing those activities and, more importantly, how they felt.

EMBRACE AMBIGUITY AND CHAOS AND QUESTION EVERYTHING

My diagnosis for recovery and pain relief were the definition of ambiguous, which immediately triggered chaotic feelings that weren't going away anytime soon. It's easy to get lost in that chaos and feel hopeless. Embracing it allows you to organize that chaos by asking questions. I questioned the doctor's ambiguous recovery diagnosis. I know that experts hedge. It's how they survive and even thrive as experts, especially when their data comes from the general population.

> When you find experiences in life that provide you mental relief and immense happiness, you're willing to do almost anything to get back to it.

The ordinary. Ordinary people get lost in chaos and don't have a footing to question experts. Unordinary people question everything. That's how Joel was able to survive his cancer diagnosis and how I recovered from my crash.

CHANNEL YOUR GRIT AND DETERMINATION AND DO WHAT'S HARD

It would have been easy to feel sorry for myself. But during the many months of my recovery, I only felt sorry for myself once. I stopped taking my pain medicine well before my intense pain went away. My doctor told me they couldn't guarantee my pain would ever go away. I remember lying in the fetal position and thinking I couldn't handle this intense pain for the rest of my life. After an hour, I forced myself up and began doing my physical therapy, which provided some relief from my pain.

That day, I did over six hours of physical training. I did the eight recommended at-home exercises my therapist gave me over and over and over. Eventually, the pain went away. I did over four hours of physical training and every therapy I could find each day from that point forward—hyperbaric chamber, cryotherapy, infrared sauna, ultraviolet light therapy, needling, cupping, electric shock muscle stimulation, and IV drip therapies. I ate clean and focused on my sleep discipline. If the Olympics had a recovery sport, I was going to win the gold. Pain can debilitate you, or it can be a powerful motivator for action. Whether the pain is emotional or physical, it's always your choice.

OBSERVE THE IMPOSSIBLE AND UNLEARN INSTANT GRATIFICATION

After observing the impossibility of a full recovery, impatience quickly set in. That impatience allowed me to focus intensely on my recovery. However, the progress was excruciatingly slow and instant gratification elusive. So instead of looking for improvement each day, I chose to imagine that progress would be there tomorrow. The next day, it wouldn't be there, but I'd look for it tomorrow. That's how I unlearned instant gratification. It was always there, just always in the not-so-distant future. I turned instant gratification into a vision by observing the impossible.

Accessing these principles individually would have only gotten me so far. A successful recovery required me to act upon all the principles of intentional disruption at some point in the process. Understanding my different, embracing my fears, observing the impossible, and acting intentionally enabled me to take control of my recovery rather than letting my diagnosis or pain control the outcome.

Life is a game. Sometimes winning is easy, and other times it's throwing us into a traumatic, life-changing event. Either way, the gift of intentional disruption is always available. We need to control the thoughts we entertain, the judgments we make about them, and our choices. That makes finding our *Why*, embracing our fears, observing our impossible, and acting with intention easy. Good luck on your journey, and enjoy the fun, joy, and happiness it brings along the way!

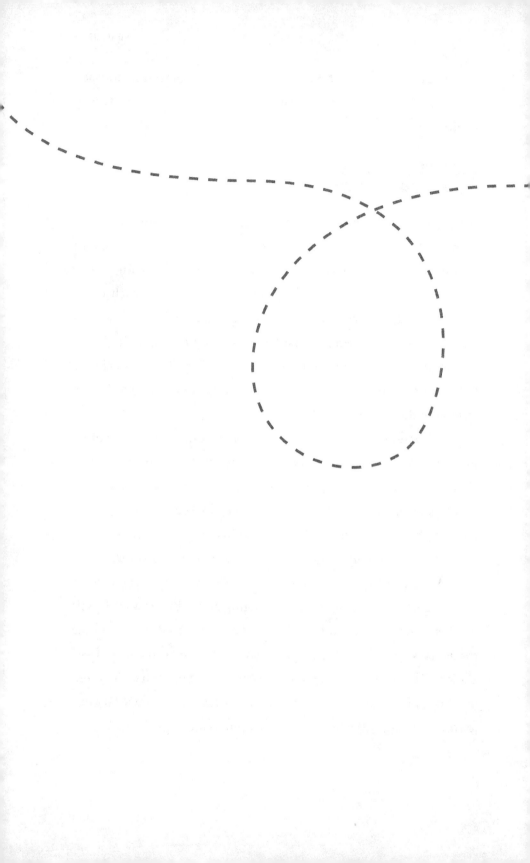

Statements of an Intentional Disruptor

On a scale of 1-5, with 1 being the least, rate your relatability to the following statements:

_____ I influence others.

_____ I achieve things others think are impossible.

_____ I don't recognize myself from five years ago.

_____ I aggressively pursue continual improvement.

_____ I am aware of my beliefs and where they've come from.

_____ I am influenced by others and what they say/think about me.

_____ I can state my *Why* in a sentence and return to it often.

_____ I spend a significant time trying to capitalize on my strengths.

_____ I can embrace failure and learn from it.

_____ I am comfortable being uncomfortable.

_____ I do not let fear impact my ability to take action.

_____ I intentionally put myself in uncomfortable situations.

_____ I am comfortable in chaotic situations and can handle ambiguity.

_____ I am curious about what's happening around me and spend significant time observing.

_____ I often dream about possibilities and practice being creative.

_____ I have an optimistic attitude, especially in difficult situations.

_____ I am resilient when I face setbacks.

_____ I gravitate toward mentally difficult situations.

_____ I do not expect instant gratification.

_____ I communicate my vision clearly and continuously.

Now add up all your responses to see how you track against the max score of 100. I recommend taking the quiz every three months. Are you continuing your journey to break away from normal by embracing your fears, observing the impossible, and acting intentionally?

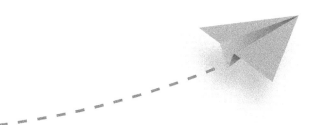

CONTACT

For more resources, plus an assessment to discover how you can become disruptable, visit disruptable.com.

And for inquiries on coaching or speaking engagements, please reach out to me directly at allan@disruptable.com.

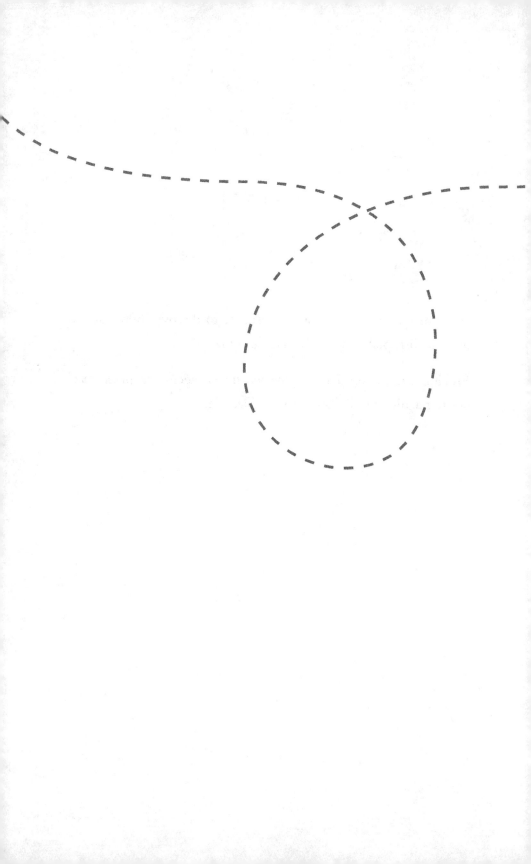

ENDNOTES

1 Avram J. Holmes and Lauren M. Patrick, "The Myth of Optimality in Clinical Neuroscience," *Trends in Cognitive Sciences* 22, no. 3 (March 1, 2018): 241–257.

2 "The World Health Report 2001: Mental Disorders affect one in four people," World Health Organization, September 28, 2001, https://www.who.int/news/item/28-09-2001-the-world-health-report-2001-mental-disorders-affect-one-in-four-people.

3 "Bipolar Disorder," National Institute of Mental Health, accessed October 22, 2021, https://www.nimh.nih.gov/health/statistics/bipolar-disorder.

4 Johan Wiklund et al., "Mental Disorders in the Entrepreneurship Context: Being Different Can Be an Advantage," *Academy of Management Perspectives* 32, no. 2 (June 13, 2018).

5 Doyle Rice, "Sharks vs. humans: At 100 million deaths against 6 each year, it's not a fair fight," USA Today, July 11, 2018, https://www.usatoday.com/story/news/2018/07/11/sharks-humans-no-fair-fight/775409002/.

6 "What are the world's deadliest animals?" BBC, June 15, 2016, https://www.bbc.com/news/world-36320744

7   "Black Friday Death Count," accessed October 22, 2021, http://black-fridaydeathcount.com/.

8   Siri Carpenter, "We don't know our own strength," American Psychological Association, October 2001, accessed June 8, 2021, https://www.apa.org/monitor/oct01/strength

9   "The Fear of Failure: Understanding the Psychology Behind It," SACAP, November 7, 2016, https://www.sacap.edu.za/blog/counselling/the-psychology-of-failure/.

10 Benjamin Hardy, "How To Become More Intelligent (According to Einstein)," Mission.org, July 2018, accessed October 22, 2021, https://medium.com/the-mission/if-youre-not-changing-as-a-person-then-you-re-not-intelligent-according-to-einstein-73ba950d99d5#:~:text=If%20you're%20seeking%20external,equipped%20to%20change%20the%20world.

11 Nattavudh Powdthavee, "Think having children will make you happy?" The Psychologist, April 2009, https://thepsychologist.bps.org.uk/volume-22/edition-4/think-having-children-will-make-you-happy.

12 "7 Incredible Studies that Prove the Power of the Mind," Power of Positivity, January 5, 2015, https://www.powerofpositivity.com/7-incredible-studies-that-prove-the-power-of-the-mind/.

13 Scott Lilienfield, "Fudge Factor: A Look at a Harvard Science Fraud Case," Scientific American, November 1, 2010, https://www.scientificamerican.com/article/fudge-factor/.

14 Srini Pillay, "Your Brain Can Only Take So Much Focus," Harvard Business Review, May 12, 2017, https://hbr.org/2017/05/your-brain-can-only-take-so-much-focus.

15 "The Purpose of Life Is Not To Be Happy But to Matter," Quote Investigator, November 29, 2014, https://quoteinvestigator.com/2014/11/29/purpose/.

16 Jenny Santi, "The Secret to Happiness Is Helping Others," accessed October 22, 2021, http://time.com/collection/ guide-to-happiness/4070299/secret-to-happiness/.

17 Benjamin P. Hardy, "3 ways people become stuck, undeveloped, and unsuccessful," November 2, 2018, https://www.theladders.com/career-advice/3-ways-people-become-stuck-undeveloped-and-unsuccessful.

18 "Grit: The Power of Passion and Perseverance," TED Talk by Angela Lee Duckworth, May 9, 2013, video, https://www.youtube.com/ watch?v=H14bBuluwB8&t=7s

19 Diane Coutu, "How Resilience Works," Harvard Business Review, May 2002, accessed June 8, 2021, https://hbr.org/2002/05/ how-resilience-works

20 David Sturt and Todd Nordstrom, "Is the Need for Instant Gratification Killing Long-Term Results? You Might Be Surprised," accessed October 22, 2021, https://www.forbes.com/sites/davidsturt/2017/09/12/is-the-need-for-instant-gratification-killing-long-term-results-you-might-be-surprised/#7ef8e3133558.

21 Jason Kottke, "If you can't explain something in simple terms, you don't understand it," Kottke.org, June 15, 2017, https://kottke.org/17/06/if-you-cant-explain-something-in-simple-terms-you-dont-understand-it.

CPSIA information can be obtained
at www.ICGtesting.com
Printed in the USA
BVHW041753131022
649397BV00004B/6/J